GROW
YOURSELF
BEAUTIFUL

GROW
YOURSELF
BEAUTIFUL

A Smart Girl's Guide to Following Her
Heart and Focusing on Her Inner Joy

— SHARON CALDWELL PEDDIE —

 iUniverse®

GROW YOURSELF BEAUTIFUL
A SMART GIRL'S GUIDE TO FOLLOWING HER
HEART AND FOCUSING ON HER INNER JOY

iUniverse books may be ordered through booksellers or by contacting:

iUniverse
1663 Liberty Drive
Bloomington, IN 47403
www.iuniverse.com
1-800-Authors (1-800-288-4677)

Because of the dynamic nature of the Internet, any web addresses or links contained in this book may have changed since publication and may no longer be valid. The views expressed in this work are solely those of the author and do not necessarily reflect the views of the publisher, and the publisher hereby disclaims any responsibility for them.

Any people depicted in stock imagery provided by Getty Images are models, and such images are being used for illustrative purposes only. Certain stock imagery © Getty Images.

The people depicted on the cover are the 3 daughters of the author. Photograph was taken by and is the property of Sharon Caldwell Peddie.

ISBN: 978-1-5320-5734-2 (sc)
ISBN: 978-1-5320-5736-6 (hc)
ISBN: 978-1-5320-5735-9 (e)

Library of Congress Control Number: 2018911507

Print information available on the last page.

iUniverse rev. date: 10/05/2018

Endorsements

"Sharon's beautiful book drew me in immediately with her positive, creative and nurturing voice. Truly, Sharon's heart shines through. She gives understanding and loving guidance to girls who are becoming women, leaving them and their parents with comfort in a confused culture. As I read each chapter, I wanted each of my own daughters to share in Sharon's beautiful message: A feeling that we are collectively all in this together!"
-Pamela Havey Lau, Author of *A Friend In Me: How to be a Safe Haven for Other Women,* Communications Professor at George Fox University, Inspirational Public Speaker and mom of 3 daughters.

"In my practice as a Pediatrician, I have the opportunity to work with many young women who regularly express the struggles they face. It's always nice to read books like this that can offer them practical, joyful ways to build their inner strength and resiliency needed in today's world."
-Laura L. Dahl, MD, FAAP

"Being a dad of 3 girls of different ages and personalities, I read this book through 3 different lens. I found valuable, experienced guidance for all of them. I even found some for myself!"
-Mitch M., Athletic footwear, Apparel & Equipment Exec.

"As a teacher, coach, and mentor over the past 20 years I believe this book has wonderful advice and guidance for all young women who are navigating the world. This book made me think about ways I can grow myself beautiful!

-Ryann Furrer

"Having a lot of experience with kids as a middle and high school track and cross country coach, volunteer and youth mentor at schools for 20+ years and even as a mom of 3 boys, I feel Sharon's words of guidance are both comforting and reassuring; not just valuable for girls and young women, they're valuable for all of us and can be used as a reference at any age. It's not a book you'll pack away or put on a shelf for dust."

-Tammy Austin

Grow Yourself Beautiful ...

Grow yourself away from society's harmful pressures.
Grow yourself away from chasing perfection.
Grow yourself away from worrying so much about outer beauty.
Grow yourself away from unrealistic
expectations for you to overachieve.
Grow yourself away from anxiety and stress.
Grow yourself away from negativity.
Grow yourself away from being rushed
through your growth journey.
Grow yourself away from worrying that you are not enough.

Grow a strong sense of self.
Grow yourself by empowering yourself.
Grow yourself in ways that make you feel good.
Grow yourself in ways that mean something to you.
Grow yourself in ways that will mean something to the world.
Grow yourself in ways that will bring you more joy.
Grow yourself in *kindness*.
Grow yourself in your *education*.
Grow yourself in *authenticity*.
Grow yourself by getting to know yourself, your
values, and your dreams by *unplugging*.
Grow yourself by living with *thanks and gratitude*.
Grow yourself in *resilience*.
Grow yourself with *faith and hope*.
Grow yourself by learning how to really *care for yourself*.
Grow yourself by learning to really *love yourself*.
Grow yourself by sharing your *love with the world*.
Grow yourself in inner strength and true beauty.
Grow yourself beautiful!

#growyourselfbeautiful

I dedicate this book to you, my loving, *beautiful* daughters, Kelsey, Kendall, and Cameron. I love being your mom more than I could ever write in words! Our bond means the world to me and will always be my greatest, most treasured accomplishment. It may sound funny to you, but in many ways, I feel we have all helped raise each other. You have helped me grow as a person just as much as I've helped you. Together, we have learned so much about ourselves. At the top of that list is that we've learned the way we feel about ourselves on the inside is really the key to our joy. Therefore, that's where we should each continue our love, focus, and work on our life's journey.

I'm so grateful that you have always trusted me with your thoughts and feelings. That is a beautiful gift you have given me and something I will always honor and protect. Because of your trust, strength, and courage to come to me for help and guidance when needed, we've been able to get through anything and everything together. Our close relationship has always lightened our loads and multiplied our joys. I love you each as the unique and special people you are. I also love our squad we make up together. You're my best friends and my heart.

I hope we will always take the love we're so blessed to have with each other and share it with all the girls and women in our lives and on our paths, especially when they need help on their journeys, just as we often need ourselves. You are so meaningfully *beautiful*— keep growing yourselves *beautiful!*

Love, Mom

B-E-A-U-T-I-F-U-L
Contents

Preface

Girls today carry a pretty heavy load of pressures from society that many don't even realize. Our society aggressively feeds our girls harmful messages, beginning at a very early age—pushing unrealistic standards for outer-beauty perfection and high expectations of overachievement for just about all areas of their lives. Those pressures feel very defeating to young girls and are destructive to their self-esteem, potential, and overall joy of life. Seemingly overnight, too many go from being happy and confident little girls to being highly stressed, anxious, and often depressed young women, doubting they are enough or can ever be enough.

The important transition from girl to young woman is a fragile journey and should be recognized as one. *Grow Yourself Beautiful* acknowledges the journey and its pressures and encourages girls to take time to build a strong sense of self and foundation needed for life. *Grow Yourself Beautiful* provides comforting advice on how girls can shift focus away from the stressful and unrealistic expectations and empower themselves to move focus in a more positive, joyful, and meaningful direction.

With an empowered, strong sense of self, they will care less about what the world tells them they need to be and grow more confident to become who they want to be.

Introduction

I can still picture you as a little girl in your pink satin and shimmery tulle princess dress, twirling around in the kitchen, feeling like the most beautiful girl in the world. The other beautiful, bold image that comes to mind is you running around the playground in your imaginary superhero cape. You were so confident, assuring your friends that your extraordinary strength and bravery could save you all from the evils of the world!

My heart has been hurting, remembering you as that little girl. How you went from that strong, beautiful superhero princess to a young woman who lost so much confidence in your beauty and strength caught me off guard and puzzled me.

I know that you now worry so much about your physical appearance and that society's constant messages of perfection have hurt your self-esteem. I know that every time your body changes, your skin breaks out, or your hair has a mind of its own, it eats away at your self-confidence. I understand that you constantly worry if your body type is okay and if you're pretty enough or thin enough. I know you're worried about what you wear at school and out with friends.

I know that if you don't get straight As, you feel like a failure even when you've given it everything you've got. I know you're afraid to raise your hand anywhere because the world is so harsh on the wrong answer. I know you worry whether teachers and professors like you. I know how stressed you are to finish all your homework and to take tests. I know you worry if you'll get into a good college and if you can handle the college you've gotten into. I know you worry you won't measure up to your siblings in your parents', teachers', or coaches' eyes.

I know that girls can be very cruel to each other and how sad, lonely, and isolated they have made you feel at times. I know fitting in with other girls is how you measure your social success.

I know once boys are introduced into your life, it's one more thing to make you doubt you're enough.

Even though you're young, I know you worry about money. I know you worry about things you think you're supposed to have. I know you worry about family struggles.

I know that you feel tremendous pressure to excel at everything—looks, school, sports, community, activities, talents, relationships, friendships, and so on—and that everything everywhere feels like a competition. I know some parents get caught up in this early-age overachievement culture without them even realizing.

I know all these super-charged, super-competitive demands each require a lot of your time, but no one respects the whole pie of expectations or gives you adequate time to get everything done. I know this leaves you feeling like you have no control over your time management. I know you're exhausted and don't feel like you have enough time to sleep.

I know that your hormones give you many moods, headaches, and stomachaches, leaving you feeling out of sorts on many days. I know that you are faced with more and different social pressures than previous generations. I know that technology plays a huge role in whether you feel safe, popular, or liked. I know you have social pressures to drink, do drugs, and have sex younger than ever before.

I know you feel that everyone expects you to already *be be be,* and it makes you feel constantly late to life.

I know that you feel like you're supposed to flower and society hasn't given you enough time, water, or sunshine to help you establish your strong roots needed for our world. I know the world aggressively tells you who you're supposed to be and it leaves you feeling like you're not enough.

I know you have every one of these tabs open all day long and you worry about all of them. I know you need to talk and to have someone understand. I know you need to relieve this pressure but you're often afraid to admit these feelings to anyone.

You are not alone; every young woman is as worried as you are.

How do I know? I've been a mom for twenty-five years. I have raised three daughters. Because of my three daughters, I've also spent a great amount of time with their friends, who have felt like my daughters too. In addition, I've spent over twenty years volunteering and working closely with young women, ages five to eighteen-plus years old, in many different capacities. I have worked with girls in schools; Girl Scouts; dance teams; soccer, volleyball, and basketball teams; churches; community services; leadership development programs; and sororities. I have been blessed to spend a tremendous amount of time with precious young women like you. I've seen, heard, and experienced firsthand how overwhelmed many of you feel. You don't have to tell me; I see you and I feel you. It has made me want to help you.

We live in a country where women are very fortunate to have many freedoms and opportunities, so people in our country find it hard to understand our culture of overachievement and our superficial focus on looks cause you so much stress. I know if we asked you, you would say most times you feel anything but free. So many messages are bombarding you as to what you should be, achieve, and look like. These messages to you started at such an early age—and have been relentless ever since.

Messages of physical beauty and perfection always seem to come to the forefront, and more things keep getting added to the superficial perfection list. It's not just unrealistic; it's become extremely overwhelming to you, so much so there are way too many of you plagued with anxiety, depression, sleep issues, bullying, overeating, undereating, underage drinking, and drug use ... or just an inability to experience life's simple joys!

This is a time in your life when you should get to feel free and excited about your future. Instead, our culture has you living in a constant state of high-level stress. You are our country's beautiful young future, and you shouldn't have to feel this way. It's all so counterproductive to your beautiful growth and potential. We need to you to be strong. We need you to feel good about you.

Thank goodness for the parents and people in your life who do try to counteract these harmful messages. Thank goodness they try to encourage you to not give so much merit to these expectations. However, in my experience, I've learned from listening to and observing you that it's not enough for us to tell you not to worry about all of this. I've learned that our shielding words to you are only temporarily comforting and not convincing enough for you to truly believe in yourself.

Without my daughters realizing it, they have helped me understand, and that's what this book is all about. The way you feel about yourself—not what we encourage you to feel about yourself—is the key to your inner peace, confidence, comfort, and joy. For you to truly *feel* beautiful, strong, and capable, you have to build and believe this about yourself. We all absolutely need our personal cheerleaders and support systems in our lives, but the way you feel about yourself is what will make or break your happiness.

You've been so rushed by our society; you haven't really been given the chance or a fair amount of time to decide what you think true beauty, strength, and success look like.

As you read this book, I hope you will begin to unload your burden. Let's work together to help shift your focus away from these pressures that cause you so much stress and move it toward learning about you and building you. It's a journey and not something that happens overnight, so let yourself take a long, deep breath and begin to relax. Let's begin to peel away those old thoughts and help you empower yourself to *grow yourself beautiful*—the kind of beautiful that makes you feel good.

Let's explore and grow in the word B-E-A-U-T-I-F-U-L, one letter and one chapter at a time.

One

The most beautiful and powerful women in the world are not physically perfect; they're kind.

Grow Yourself **B**-E-A-U-T-I-F-U-L
B Is for Being Kind
Kindness Is Beautiful

Sometimes we're the person in need of kindness. Sometimes we're the person who gets the opportunity to show kindness to others. In both situations, kindness makes everyone involved feel something beautiful, powerful, and warm.

Did you know all kinds of studies show we feel happier and more positive when we show kindness to other people? Kindness studies show that practicing kindness can actually improve our overall wellbeing. When we're kind, we feel emotionally warm inside, and that releases chemicals in our brain that reduce our blood pressure and stress. That's an awesome, wonderful relationship. If you share your kindness with others, it will return happiness and health benefits to you! I've included a few resources at the back of this book incase you'd like to explore the scientific relationship a bit more.

Have you ever noticed that sincerely kind people have a certain beauty that radiates and shines all over them? As you empower yourself to grow a strong foundation of who you are, I hope you'll think about embracing the beauty and power of sincere kindness. Just like love, kindness is at the core of humanity and is such a powerful world changer. Kindness has the power to change the big world, someone else's world, and your personal world! Kindness is something every human being needs and can relate to. Kindness is something you can easily show to make someone else's world a more beautiful, safe, and comfortable place—and a wonderful way for that person to do the same for you in return. You can build yourself with the positive power that kindness brings!

Society would like you to think beauty is all about the exterior. Everywhere you turn, there seem to be messages and advertisements for products trying to convince you that you need them in order to be beautiful. That isn't fair to you because true beauty is really about someone's inner light. Kindness is such a huge part of that beautiful inner light. It's a beauty product that you don't need to purchase. Kindness doesn't cost a thing. Kind people are so beautiful without putting one thing on their face or body!

Think of all the people you've had in your life. It's not usually how they look that made you care about them; it's the kindness they've shared with you. Think back to the normal anxiety you had before a first day of school, or a first day on a team or a job—or any new experience. I bet if you look back on those situations, you'll see someone's kindness eased that anxiety for you and brought you comfort. Maybe it was a smile, or someone just taking the time to show you how to get where you were going. Maybe it was that tip on how to deal with a difficult coach, player, or teacher. Maybe it was that one girl who invited you to sit at the lunch table when no one else acknowledged you needed a friend and a place to sit. We all have that power to make someone else's world a better one through our kindness.

Think of all the interactions we have throughout a day. If we begin our day within our own home, being the kind of family members who look out for and treat each other with kindness, kindness can then spill out from us to the people we encounter in our everyday world. Think of the people who hold open doors for us, or the people who let them slam in our face, and how that makes you feel. Think of the people who let us merge onto the road, and then those determined to selfishly cut us off so they move ahead by three seconds. Take a moment and think of the circles of people you come in contact with all day and how those interactions make or break your day for you. They leave you feeling either comforted or uncomfortable, loved or unloved, respected or disrespected. Kindness impacts everyone's sense of security. Kindness or a lack of it definitely has an impactful ripple effect, so why aren't people more aware it and practicing more kindness?

THE GIRL WORLD CAN BE REALLY UNKIND

I've talked about kindness in a general sense, but I think it's really important to address how much we need more kindness within our female world since that will always be a big part of your immediate world. Kindness from girls or the lack of it either makes or breaks your day. It's not a fun fact, but girls and women cause each other a tremendous amount of stress and heartache. Girls can be very unkind to each other. I wish I could say it's not something you will have to deal with once you get into adult friendships and the female working world, but it is. It's a harsh reality to live with, but many females compete with and judge each other, rather than lift and support.

So why are girls and women so unkind to each other? It usually falls somewhere in the categories of jealousy, insecurity, competition, control, social hierarchy, retaliation, attention, and life troubles. So much acknowledgment is given to boys bullying other boys. However, girls and women can be much worse to each other. They judge, gossip, harass, humiliate, exclude, and isolate. Social media has made torturing each other with these unkind behaviors even more prevalent.

What makes this so painful is females really need their girlfriends. I know if you don't feel you're doing well among other girls, it doesn't matter how many other things are going well. You feel miserable, right? We really need our girl world to be going well for us in order to feel well. If you're a girl, then I know you've been the recipient of some sort of mean, unhealthy, unkind girl behavior. I know it has caused you a lot of pain and has really harmed your self-esteem.

Since this is such prevalent behavior and we've acknowledged how much our female relationships mean to us, we must try to grow better and kinder to each other. We need to positively influence this painful climate. Some girls and women will always be "mean girls," and I believe it's because they don't work on themselves. They are the ones not growing their lives in ways that they're proud of and that feel good to them. Maybe they don't want to put in the work. Maybe they just don't know how. We can't change them or their lives until they're ready, but we can grow ourselves in beautiful and kind ways that will ensure we will not become unkind like them. They can't feel good about themselves or their lives until they grow in ways they're proud of, and maybe you can set the example by the way you grow. If you work on yourself and grow yourself in beautiful, kind, meaningful ways, you will grow in your security and confidence and won't be someone who needs to put others down in order to feel good. That is a beautiful gift to yourself and a beautiful example to them!

Just as mean girls become less attractive, girls who have kind hearts become more beautiful. Try to become more aware of the dynamics of your girl circles and how you all treat each other. I hope you'll always stay determined to not be the bully. Bullies are not attractive. Some people never see that about themselves, but I hope you'll take the time to self-reflect. I hope you'll remain determined to never become the bully's weak or devoted follower either. Sometimes it's hard to see if you are a passive bully by being a follower. Be aware of that, because that role is just as harmful and hurtful to others as being the queen bee of the bullying. Being a passive follower of a bully is not attractive.

Be a leader, and be the most kindhearted girl in your circle. Your kindness can help ward off a lot of destructive competition. Your kindness can help make insecure girls feel less threatened and create a safer climate for you and for everyone. Your kindness brings healthy energy to your female group.

You will begin to see that kindness automatically makes people softer toward you. It takes some time for the tougher situations with the tougher girls to get sorted out. But, if you can be patient, be kind, and not overreact, you'll see that your kindness can get you gracefully through so much of that. Insecure mean girls may still exclude you, gossip about you, and hurt you. Find comfort and power in knowing that beautiful, kind girls end up having the most meaningful friendships in the long run. If you're a beautifully kind girl, you will attract healthy, beautifully kind girls to be your true friends. You'll see that. Keep growing yourself toward kindness and away from unkind relationships and unkind girls. Also, find comfort and your power in knowing that unkind girls, regardless of how they appear, never get to feel beautiful inside. They really don't. Keep growing yourself in ways that will make you feel beautiful inside. Being a kind girl in an unkind girl world will make you feel amazingly powerful and beautiful.

Grow yourself beautiful.

BE THE KIND OF KIND PERSON YOU ADMIRE

Whether in your girl world or in the big world, I hope you'll keep growing in kindness so you can admire yourself as much as or more than you would anyone else. Others will admire you for your kindness and beauty too. Too often, girls spend time admiring and comparing themselves to other people only to learn they weren't worth the pain of comparison. Over the years, I have admired various friends, teachers, business associates, fellow volunteers, celebrities, politicians, and so on. I have thought they were beautiful in appearance or admired their résumé or persona. At a closer look, once I knew them for a period of time, I reluctantly had to see them in a different light. I wanted them to be as beautiful, kind, or impressive as they appeared, but after some time, I was forced to see how they lacked a genuine kindness toward others. I believe it's hard for any of us to truly find someone impressive or beautiful if he or she doesn't treat others with kindness. I want to encourage you to focus on who you are, rather than on comparisons. If you do this, you will never waste your time, and you will become the person you admire most. You will know your kindness is authentic for sure, and that feels so beautiful.

I really want to encourage you to look beyond outer beauty and superficial impressions before you torture yourself aspiring to be or look like someone else. Keep empowering yourself to grow in ways where you feel authentically beautiful, strong, and impressive to yourself. Kindness is the road to that!

The beautiful thing about kindness is it's so easy to get started with in your life. Kindness requires no prerequisite. You don't have to "be" anything already to practice it and to touch others with it. There is no class you need to take first. There isn't a special talent you need to have been born with. There is no special skill you need to perfect first. All you have to do is begin treating others the way you want and need to be treated yourself.

I've heard people say kindness is a weakness. What?! I could not disagree more. Unkind people are usually unkind because they feel weak and powerless in a situation. Kindness is a very powerful feeling, and people who show kindness have a strength and beauty that cannot be denied. As you develop in your kindness, you will begin to feel people respond to your "kindness beauty". They will respond to you in positive ways because "kindness beauty" is something that shines all around you and back onto you! People are so in need of kindness that you will feel loved and be loved even more when it becomes a natural part of you and the way you do life. It really will cultivate a *beautiful aura and dynamic* for yourself and all around you. It may seem too simple. It may seem like something you already know and not that big of a deal. However, if you become really aware of kindness and share it more than you ever have, the way you feel about yourself will become very beautiful and powerful. The positive effects of kindness will bring so much more joy to your life! Test it out; feel its effects. Kindness is beauty and magic you can create.

Here are just a few beautiful and powerful ways to share kindness.

- Start being kinder to yourself. Make a list of ways to be kind to you, and act on them.
- Smile at people.
- Hug often.
- Put away your phone for someone, and listen to him or her. Really listen.
- Call someone to let him or her know he or she is special to you.
- Do something for someone who is having a hard time.
- Do something for someone who isn't having a hard time; it will help that person keep his or her smile.
- Show good old-fashioned manners; respect and manners show kindness.
- Say thank you often! Being grateful is kind.
- Try to empathize more. See people's lives through their eyes, not through your eyes.

- Include others more. You would be surprised how many people feel left out or alone.
- When you're part of a moving group, wait for someone who's lagging behind to catch up.
- Don't be a bully. Don't passively follow a bully. Don't even bully a bully.
- Don't judge people. Don't judge yourself!
- Don't participate in gossip.
- Lift people up. Lift yourself up too!
- Uplift and connect positively with others when using social media.
- Give many sincere compliments, even to strangers.
- Donate money, clothes, food, or whatever you can.
- Lend with generosity.
- Put away something that someone else took out of it's place
- Pick up a piece of trash regardless of who left it.
- Love your animal. Pet or show love to someone else's animal.
- Offer people a piece of your gum.
- Be helpful.
- Hold a door for someone.
- Be a really good, genuine friend.
- Celebrate other people's achievements and successes.
- Practice random acts of kindness in all areas of your life.
- Be a woman who lifts and supports other women.
- When kindness doesn't work in a situation, show kindness to yourself by moving on.

Those are just a few ideas to get you thinking; however, you will have many interactions and opportunities throughout your day to practice kindness.

As you reflect and grow in your kindness, think about one more thing—kindness toward everyone. Try not to be "selectively kind."

Don't reserve kindness for people you think deserve it and withhold it from people you feel are undeserving or don't need it. Whether or not you can always see it, we all have life happening to us. Everyone is in need of kindness. This doesn't mean you should tolerate unkind people in your life. You absolutely should not. Just kindly walk away. That's a kind thing to do for you. It makes a kinder life for you.

Put yourself at the top of your "be kind to" list. Please make it a priority and way of life to be kind to yourself! You are worthy of every single kind word or act you would give someone else. Keep reminding yourself to not think bad thoughts about you or treat yourself in an unkind way. This is very important to growing yourself beautiful. Be gentle with yourself. Recognize your heart, your strengths, and how hard you try in life, and practice kind thoughts about you. Being kind to you can make or break your day and the way you're feeling. It will make or break your life. Practice saying sincere, kind things to yourself. Practice doing kind, nurturing things for yourself. Make time to make yourself feel special. Smile at yourself! Compliment yourself! Put the world away sometimes and kindly listen to your heart. Listening to yourself helps you grow and establish a strong sense of who you are.

Kindness to yourself and others will attract beautiful circumstances and people toward you. Kindness is beautiful. Wouldn't you agree that kind people grow more and more beautiful to us as we get to know them? When you grow yourself in kindness and get to know yourself as a kind person, you really will feel more beautiful and strong. The way you feel about yourself is the key to your joy.

Kindness is beautiful. Grow yourself kind.

Grow yourself beautiful.

Two

The most beautiful and powerful women in the world did not all get straight As, but they all value education and hard work.

Grow Yourself B-**E**-A-U-T-I-F-U-L
E Is for Education and Empowerment
An Educated Woman Is Beautiful

It's hard to believe, but women in many parts of the world are denied the right to get an education. Have you ever sat back and thought about what your life might be like if you were born in another country? What if you were born in a country that doesn't value educating women? What if suddenly you were told that girls in America were no longer allowed to be educated and that your role in society didn't matter enough to let you have an education? Let that sink in for a minute. How dare someone think you are not worth educating? How does that make you feel?

How lucky you are to live in a country that does believe in educating women. I know with school pressures, it may not feel like a privilege sometimes. It's heartbreaking that somewhere along the way, American education has forced students and teachers to become so driven by grades and test scores that many of you have lost your joy of learning. With that emphasis, it's no wonder you feel stressed out. It's no wonder so many feel if you don't get straight As, you're a failure. Who can feel that getting an education is a privilege when there is so much focus and stress on grades, grades, grades! And scores, scores, scores!

At the moment, if you're a student, there isn't much you can do about education in America being so grade and test score oriented. It's my hope we can bring awareness to how counterproductive and harmful it is to put so much pressure and focus on grades and scores. However, what you can do is empower yourself to try to radically shift your focus from getting good grades and scores to becoming an educated woman. Becoming an educated woman equals knowledge, independence, and power.

Remember when you were little and you followed your mom and dad around and wanted to learn anything and everything? You wanted to know, "Why does this do this? What is that for?" You were curious, and it was fun to learn, because you faced no ominous pressure about a grade. You wanted to learn to put on your own shoes. You wanted to touch piano keys to hear the sound they made. You wanted to know how much the coins on your parents' dresser added up to. You were excited to learn. You wanted to get educated about everything so you could be smart and in charge of yourself. That knowledge allowed you independence from other people you needed to do things for you. You felt so excited, proud, and powerful ... remember?

What if you started to think about education in that way again, instead of stressing about getting straight As? Do you think you really need straight As to become well educated and make valuable contributions to yourself, your family, your community, or society? Isn't knowledge what you're really after? Isn't knowledge what you've always been after? Being an educated woman will always make you feel proud, safe, independent, powerful, and beautiful! Being an educated woman will also make you feel strong and more likely to live a healthy, thriving life. That's what you want for yourself, right? I don't know any young woman who wouldn't want that. So how about we try to concentrate on just that? Let's go after the knowledge! Empower yourself to be educated and strive for excellence, not perfection. It's very, very possible and even probable that amazing grades will be a *natural* result of that. Let's shift focus to the part that feels good, and that's being a well-educated, knowledgeable woman.

In America, you get to be anything you want to be, but even the magnitude of that statement can sometimes feel overwhelming. So many messages expect you to already know what you want to be even though you are just developing as a person. So many messages expect you to want to become president just because that's one of your freedoms. That statement in and of itself can feel stressful at a young age. Besides, maybe you're supposed to do something more spiritual or artistic; our world needs many different kinds of contributions. Yes, you love the message you can be anything you want to be, but let's let you decide in your own time what feels good to you. The world needs to stop talking to you about becoming a future world leader before you've even learned how to get along with other kids on the playground. How about we let you have a chance to understand what's going on in your government class before we have you going to Washington? Or how about we let you have time to develop your courage to just run for a school class office before expecting you to someday become president of the United States? Sheesh, first things first. Let's help you build a strong foundation for yourself before we push you so hard to start overachieving! Freedom to become anything you want to be is indeed a beautiful privilege, but overzealous parents and society need to let you grow first. Pushing so hard and so early causes you a lot of anxiety and steals your love of learning. We don't want that ominous pressure of these way-too-early, unrealistic expectations to sidetrack you from your natural full potential.

Remember, the idea of this book is *growing* yourself. You shouldn't have to know what you want to be at a young age. You shouldn't have to already be on some kind of fast track to greatness! It's okay to tell people you are learning about many different things and you will get back to them on what your heart tells you to follow. Empower yourself to believe in this different, more relaxed mindset. Just moving your concentration to educating yourself will give you so many choices and open so many doors, when you are ready to open them.

Just take it a day at a time, and remember and *feel* the fun of learning anything and everything your heart desires. Each time you learn something, not only are you becoming more educated and stronger, you're building your independence. You feel more beautiful because you are feeling and becoming capable and powerful—and that's what we should really want for you.

I really do believe you will feel much less anxiety and stress about school once you empower yourself to stop chasing perfect grades and replace that with your desire to chase knowledge. Having this kind of focus with a more relaxed approach will bring you greater success in school. You'll make your learning process more about you. You've always wanted learn.

We all have different subjects that we're interested in. You only have a few years of your life that school tells you what you have to learn. I know some subjects are very boring. Some subjects seem like a waste of time and like information you'll probably never use. Just empower yourself to work harder when you don't find something particularly interesting, knowing someday you will get to pursue the subjects you are most interested in. Even if it doesn't seem a subject will play a direct role in your future, I hope you can find some comfort and inspiration in knowing that every subject at least teaches you how to learn. It primes you to be able and ready to learn that special something that will make an exciting impact in your life. Working hard, especially on something that is not your favorite, is a beautiful quality to have!

Think about embracing this too. Instead of feeling stressed about hard work, empower yourself to let hard work make you feel beautiful and strong! This isn't easy, and you must put in strong effort. Feel your strength and beauty in your hard work. You are doing this for you. You're creating your great future—and you deserve it.

To help you embrace this new way of thinking, I want to share one of my favorite heartwarming and empowering thoughts regarding educating girls and women. History has taught us that when we educate a woman, we educate a nation. I've always loved the power for women in that thought. Let's think about the meaning of educating a woman and what it's taught us. Educated women understand their rights. Educated women can have great jobs that make great contributions to their society. The income of an educated woman allows her to not depend on anyone else to provide for her. She doesn't have to go anywhere she doesn't want to. Educated women have learned how to protect themselves and keep themselves physically safe. Educated women know how to live a healthy life.

Educated women can lead and influence our government. Educated women lift up their nations as a whole because of all that they know and everyone they touch. Many of you will be moms, if you choose to be, or have opportunities to work with and be around young people. If you are educated, you will naturally inspire young people to get educated too. You will share your knowledge with your own kids as you raise them or others as you work with them. Your knowledge will make you so valuable to your families and communities.

Isn't it cool to think about that as you become educated, you will lift up everyone around you? You will lift up you, your family, your community, your nation, and the world just by having contact with them—just by being you! Education teaches you to live a prosperous, healthier, happier life and help any people who cross your path do the same just by what you know. Who knew you would have such power just by becoming an educated woman!

As you have already experienced, the path to becoming a well-educated woman is not an easy one. I want you to give yourself this gift by remembering not all people have the same exact capacity to learn the exact same things in the exact same way in the exact same environment. We're all different, and we all learn differently. That's not bad. That's another cool thing that makes us unique! Let's celebrate that! It's sad that so many aren't smart enough to know that's actually something cool and special. You are smart enough to celebrate that about you! Also, not everyone is wired to be "academic" and "scholastic," but that doesn't mean you can't be good at learning or you're not bright or powerful. Grades will probably always be the measurement of success for school, but that doesn't mean that's the measure of whether you will succeed in life. Please hold on to that forever.

You always want to put yourself in a position to make your own choices and not have them decided for you. Good grades will help keep you in the driver's seat. You don't want bad grades to determine where you get to advance or not advance. However, after trying your very best, if you don't get the grades you want, please remember there are many traits that make up a successful person. Having straight As doesn't ensure someone will be a success in life, and not having straight As doesn't mean you can't be a great success.

The next time someone impresses you, ask questions or research his or her history. Very successful people were not necessarily straight-A students. Now, I'm not encouraging you to not strive for excellence or work hard to your full potential. You should always strive for excellence and work hard for yourself. That's how you show yourself you care about you.

What I am encouraging is that you shift your stress about grades to focus on educating yourself. I encourage you to keep developing a strong work ethic, always trying hard to reach your maximum potential. After doing that, if you don't always get the grades you want, please remind yourself that it doesn't mean you're not bright, imaginative, curious, ambitious, intelligent, emotionally intelligent, resilient, optimistic, talented, motivated, passionate, hardworking, or focused. It does not mean you will be a failure. You possess many of those successful traits, so try your best to not live stressed out about grades—and switch the focus to growing your powerful traits.

Remind yourself of your many qualities and talents because that is where you will gain your strength and confidence. Those traits and qualities will be the launching pad for your future success and will make it all feel more natural. We all apply ourselves in different ways with different things and at different times in our lives. Keep remembering you are an individual. Keep reminding yourself this grade thing is temporary in the big picture of your life!

I know it's really hard, but try your best to relax. It's too hard to learn important things when you feel stressed. If you care to be, you will become educated in the things that are right for you and right for your future. No need to worry so much. You will make contributions to the world. You will have many of them—I promise you.

It's helpful and comforting to look at this knowing we're not all designed to become the same thing. The world has many needs. We don't need a world of all the same profession; that wouldn't make any sense at all. We don't need everyone to be a doctor, nurse, lawyer, astronaut, teacher, painter, professional athlete, composer, banker, rock star, chef, landscaper, yoga instructor, and so on. Everyone has a purpose, and we need you to be you. You are designed to be one of the many wonderful things our world needs. Give yourself time to grow into that. Keep adding to your education and growing your work ethic, and your star will shine. It will shine because it's yours and it fits and feels right to you. It will shine because you've invested in yourself by growing your education. Empower yourself to find the beauty and strength in being educated.

In addition to educating yourself in academics, I hope you will value educating yourself in ways that will feed and inspire you physically, emotionally, and spiritually. Taking time to learn those lessons will restore and replenish you rather than stress and drain you. A smart woman knows educating herself improves her whole being.

Whatever level of school you're in, I hope you will try to relax more so you can enjoy a lifelong journey of learning. Try your best to adopt the philosophy that being in school isn't about being perfect; it's about learning. So just keep showing up and trying your best. You'll even learn that when you show up, some of your most important lessons at school will not even be found in your books. I'm excited for you to get back in touch with that smart, curious little girl. She's still there. She'll always be there. She's right inside you. Remember how she loves to learn.

An educated woman is powerful and beautiful.

Grow yourself beautiful.

Three

The most beautiful and powerful
women in the world are authentic.

Grow Yourself B-E-**A**-U-T-I-F-U-L
A Is for Authenticity
Authenticity Is Beautiful

Authenticity is powerful and beautiful but involves time for self-discovery and the development of courage to be yourself.

We are authentic when we are in touch with who we are and what we believe in—and feel the comfort needed to expose ourselves not just to others but to ourselves as well. There is no better feeling than when we are allowed to be our natural, authentic selves with no fear of judgment and scrutiny. Authenticity is like being allowed to wear your most comfortable outfit all day in every situation—like a big T-shirt and soft sweatpants. When we align with our authenticity, we feel comfy and cozy, and it feels just right. When we don't, we feel like we're stuck in something binding and irritating. Often, we don't recognize it as that, so we aren't sure why we feel off; we just know we feel uncomfortable or anxious when we're not authentic.

Being authentic also means our words and actions match up with who we feel we are and what we believe. I think if I asked you, you would say you are an authentic person or at least you try to be. I think most people want to be authentic. We love authentic people because they're real and easy to be around. Authentic people feel trustworthy to us. They do what they say they will do, and they are genuinely what they show themselves to be. They're comfortable with who they are and what they believe. It's like they've given themselves permission to feel comfortable in their own skin.

Finding our authenticity takes time to self-reflect and to build our courage to show ourselves and the world exactly who we are. It's not always easy to be ourselves because stress and worry of if we're enough accompanies it. What if I show what I am? What if I show what I believe? What if I show what I'm really interested in? What if I show what I naturally look like? Does it even come close to what society tries to say I should be? I believe a lot of your anxiety comes from chasing an image of what you've been taught beauty, strength, and success should look like and then wondering if you measure up.

Yes, as the people who love you, we will tell you to just be yourself. We try to let you know that if the people you are with don't find your authentic self good enough, then they aren't the right people for you. It's a true message and an important message, but if you harshly judge yourself too, it doesn't matter how many of us tell you otherwise. It's you who has to believe in you first. It's you who has to stop judging you so harshly. It's you who needs to believe in who you are and feel it's okay to be an original, authentic you. We are all works in progress. Of course we all should keep growing ourselves toward becoming our best. But at our core, we need to feel free to be who we are. We yearn to be authentic.

I know you're probably saying, "Okay, but how do I get there? How do I learn to believe that my authentic self, inside and out, will even be good enough for me? How do I learn to believe that my authentic self is good enough to put out there for others to really see? How do I learn to believe that my authentic self is someone people will like and think is enough?" I understand why you ask all of that. It's scary and uncomfortable to be judged and scrutinized. However, no matter who you are and how wonderful you may be, there will always be people ready to judge you ... so you may as well just be yourself. It's so much less stressful than trying to be anything else.

I want to help you empower yourself to grow in your confidence and courage—to be yourself and love yourself—by really getting to know how unique and cool you are. Thinking, knowing, and feeling that you are enough is the key to your joy. So it's you we're going to work on getting to know. It's you we'll work on impressing. I know you've been living to try to please other people, but it's you who has to learn to love and impress you. Let's help you navigate through these pressures of unrealistic and superficial expectations so you can set yourself free.

This will require another shift in mindset. You will have to stop thinking you have to be perfect in everything in order to be special and enough. I hope you can find comfort on your journey to authenticity by knowing no one is perfect! No one is perfect—and strength, beauty, and success do not have one definition or one look. They have many examples everywhere and in everyone! You have no need to chase "perfect" because perfection doesn't even exist. Chasing it is like chasing a mirage. It's not real, so you'll never reach it. A superficial, unrealistic, cookie-cutter idea of perfection will always cause you stress because it's an uncatchable illusion. Perfection doesn't exist, and it's not supposed to.

Empower yourself to grow away from the mirage of perfection. Empower yourself to grow authentically into someone you love and admire starting today. It's a decision. It's a decision that will change your life. It's a decision that will set you free from torturing yourself by chasing something that isn't real or even necessary. You just thought the way you did because society told you so.

Somewhere along the way, society started aggressively pushing these superficial ideas of women that devalue the magnificence of authenticity, inner beauty, inner strength, and individual physical uniqueness that make the female so special—and so beautiful! Inner beauty, inner strength, and the ability to accept, embrace, and love your authentic self will bring you true, meaningful joy that lasts.

The first step toward growing in authenticity is figuring out who and what you are—and what you want yourself to mean. You build your strong foundation and deep roots by figuring out who and what you are. It's that foundation that gives you strength and direction through the world's storms and confusing messages. It's what dissolves your fragility. You may think you know who you are, but you have had a lot of mixed messages coming at you. You also live in a day and age when you have very little unplugged time to get to deeply know yourself authentically. We will cover the value of unplugging to grow in our next chapter. For now, just know the only way toward authenticity is spending quality time with yourself to discover the interests, values, and gifts of your mind, body, heart, and soul.

You have to take time to get to know you. Think of your journey so far. What has happened to you that has made your life happy? You will gain a lot of clarity as to who you are as you ask yourself questions and listen to your answers. What have you gone through that has caused you anxiety, sadness, and disappointment? Ask yourself what your values and beliefs are and what you'd like for them to be. What feels right to you? What feels wrong to you? Ask yourself how you feel when you are around certain people. Ask yourself how you feel about many different things. Take some time to write down your values in the back of this book on the journaling pages. Help yourself develop a clear picture of what you stand for. You'll know that when you listen to how you feel about different subjects. As you read this book, listen to your reactions on ways you can grow yourself. What parts do you relate to? What parts excite you? If you follow your answers, you will care less and less about what others look and sound like and find joy in following your heart.

If someone asked you the following question, how would you answer it?: Would you rather appear perfect or feel perfect? I hope you answered you would rather *feel* perfect than just appear perfect. Since your happiness and comfort level are based on how you feel, I hope you will keep moving toward growing in authenticity so you can rid yourself of some of the stress that comes with trying to measure up to all the superficial messages that conflict with what you really value.

If you really want to feel beautiful and powerful, you don't have to strive to be perfect; you just have to be authentic. Life will be beautiful, joyful, and very fulfilling without you or your life having to appear perfect. Perfection doesn't exist, and it doesn't because it's vanilla, superficial, and boring. The beauty is in the *real*.

Someone, or his or her circumstances, may seem perfect, but there is really no such thing. I don't want you to torture yourself any longer with chasing perfection. If you think someone or someone's life is perfect, you have to realize that's your evaluation and your perception; that's not reality. You have to free yourself from thinking that. Those thoughts misguide you and torture you. Many times, what appears as perfection has been doctored up to present its finest impression. The sooner you allow yourself to believe that fact, the happier and more relaxed you get to feel. I want you to give yourself the gift of not looking at ads and other people's social media or accomplishments and feeling that's what you should be. If you could ask them personally, many of these people would tell you that's not really their reality. They've worked hard for that "perfect" presentation. I hope you won't give it so much power, because so much of it truly is faked perfection and not realistic for any human.

You'll find so much fun, freedom, and power in embracing who you really are. I want you to feel all of that. I don't want you to spend a lifetime chasing something that doesn't exist. As you grow yourself with meaning and authenticity, you will relieve a lot of your pressures and anxiety. You will begin feeling so much more joy.

Because society bombards and overwhelms you with what it says you should strive to be, it gives you no fair time to check your "authentic perfection" inventory. Take the time to learn what is so authentically beautiful about yourself. You have special things about you that no one else possesses. Accept that others are uniquely them and that you are uniquely you. Their looks, their beings, and their accomplishments are meant for them, not you. You really have no need to chase their unique gifts, because you have your own. There's so much beauty in your individual authenticity, and that's why it's so important you begin to really understand you. Get in sync with all the very real, very beautiful things about you and your gifts.

As you try to embrace growing in your authenticity, try to reach deeply to understand and embrace the specialness of being something natural and unique. Women are not synthetic; we're natural beings and made to be unique originals. We have rare, one-of-a-kind markings and character, just like everything we see in nature, like diamonds! Anything and everything that is natural has one-of-a-kind beauty. Diamonds are a fun example because they are shiny, beautiful, and very interesting because of their unique characteristics—much like women.

It's the markings of the real, authentic diamond that give it beauty, depth, and character. Even though diamond experts call out imperfections within an authentic diamond, it shines brighter and warmer than any fake. It's because its realness makes it more interesting. The same goes for humans. Anything natural, versus anything manmade, will not be uniform or perfect. Isn't that fun to think about? It's not the perfect fake that has warmth, clarity, character, and brilliance; it's the authentic diamond with those so-called flaws and imperfections.

This is where we should throw out the words *perfect* and *imperfect* for natural things. We are natural. If something is natural, its beauty and perfection are in the originality and uniqueness. Those aren't really imperfections or flaws; those individual qualities allow it to shine and sparkle like none other. It's spectacular because it's one of a kind. You have no need to chase someone else's version of fake perfection. Spend your time polishing your one-of-a-kind natural beauty and characteristics by helping your authentic self shine through. If you can understand that an authentic diamond with so-called markings of imperfection is still more beautiful than a fake, then I hope you'll begin to understand that you are a natural being with unique, one-of-a-kind beauty. That's what makes you special.

They make fake "perfect" diamonds, but they can never be as precious, sparkly, and brilliant as the real, natural thing. A person wearing a fake diamond will never really feel it's good enough, because he or she knows it's not authentic.

Today is the day you begin to free yourself from chasing perfection and *empower* yourself to embrace your individuality and your originality. Would we really want every girl, every woman, every diamond, every cloud, every leaf, every butterfly, every body of water, every mountain, every state, every country, and everything in every category to look uniform and "perfectly the same"? Wouldn't that be really weird? Wouldn't it be strange to paint one definition of perfect beauty for each of those? Wouldn't we miss out on so much of their beauty, wisdom, and resources if we defined they must be a certain size, shape, or contents in order to be beautiful? You wouldn't agree with someone who held up a flower and said, "All flowers must be this color, shape, and size, or else it's not a beautiful flower," right? It's the same for people. Try to apply this to girls and women ... and to yourself! We come in all shapes, colors, and sizes and with our own unique markings and gifts to offer the world. We're original because that's how the creator of natural, living things intended us to be! That's how all natural things are created to be—spectacularly different!

Your beauty lies in your individual markings, your inner strength, your inner light, and your personal outer shine. Something authentic is so much more beautiful because it's real and rare and it allows us a chance to see and get to know that something special that's one of a kind—different from all the rest. You don't have to be the same as anyone else to be beautiful. You don't even have to try to be different to stand out and be beautiful. You just get to be you. You're already there. That's the way you were made.

Not only is authenticity beautiful, it's powerful, especially in people. Authentic people are especially beautiful and powerful because of the way they notice, accept, and embrace their unique qualities and gifts. Because they do, they bring us a comfort and security to do the same for ourselves. They're so real and seem to be able to laugh at themselves, share honest feelings, and make us feel safe to do the same. They have an admirable, humble confidence. They don't feel the need to compete, make fun of others, or make others feel uncomfortable. They are people we know we can trust and count on. Their actions match their words to us. How beautiful they are and how beautiful we can become if we all learn to embrace and live with authenticity. We all feel so good around authentic people. Authentic people make the world a more beautiful place.

While it may seem scary to be authentic, it's actually much scarier to try to be perfect or something we're not. You know the pressures in trying to match someone else's version of beauty or perfection. Being authentic and who you are is really much easier. It's a softer way to live. Yes, you have to grow in courage to become authentic, but your comfort and joy are worth being brave. Every time you grow in your authenticity, you will gain confidence in yourself and you will feel more centered and aligned with who you're meant to be. You will feel more grounded. Authentic people give themselves permission to follow what they feel is perfect for them. You deserve to be authentic.

As you embark on your self-discovery and growth in authenticity, you can learn what is authentic to you by listening to your body and the way you think and feel about things. When you just don't feel right about something you're feeling, something you're doing, something you're saying, or something you're wearing, it's because you aren't following what feels authentic to yourself. We all have an inner compass and voice that speaks to us and tells us when what we do or say or try doesn't match up with our authenticity. When you listen and follow, then you get in touch and in sync with your truth and your authentic self. When you're joyful and at ease, that's what's happening. You're following your authenticity.

Have you ever spent time with people and just not felt right after being with them? You left them, and you just didn't feel good. Maybe it's what they talked about or did or what you said and did around them. How many times have you blamed that on yourself? Maybe they didn't match your authentic self. It feels better to be alone than to be with people who don't match our authenticity.

How about when you've spent time with people who leave you feeling good? Whatever was done or said or not said felt really right to you. I bet it's because the things you did and the things you talked about felt real and authentic to your inner core.

Have you ever worn a pair of shorts, a dress, a pair of jeans, makeup, or shoes that you just felt uncomfortable in? Wearing this was supposed to help you look and feel beautiful and in style, but it didn't. Did you feel uncomfortable almost to the point where you wanted to cry or laugh at yourself? You felt that way because it didn't match your authentic style. You were uncomfortable because it just didn't feel like you. When you listen to that discomfort, that's your authentic self speaking to you.

On the flip side of that, have you ever worn something that other people didn't think was in style or right for them but that made you feel like a million bucks? Maybe it was a fabulous red dress, or maybe it was just that big T-shirt and soft sweatpants, but you felt so good! That felt great because you wanted to wear it and that was authentic to you. Maybe people even made fun of you at first, but you wore it with such authenticity, comfort, and confidence that you started a trend. Next time you saw them, they had *you* on because you made you look so good. ;)

Self-reflection and listening to what makes you feel good or not good are on the path to finding your authentic self. When we live in truth and what we're saying, doing, wearing, and becoming feels right, that's just us being authentic. If something doesn't feel right, keep moving from it to something that does feel right so you can feel in sync with yourself. That in-sync feeling is you matching up with your authenticity.

BE AUTHENTIC IN YOUR SOCIAL MEDIA

Since social media is a big part of today's world, and probably yours, let's talk about it in terms of authenticity. Social media can be a very superficial place and can easily contribute to taking you down a road that has you feeling bad about yourself. It can easily become a place where you feel unsafe to present your authentic self.

As silly as it may sound to say it aloud, I know that many young girls tie their value and self-worth to the amount of likes received on photos or posts. Because nothing could be further from the truth, I want you to empower yourself to look at social media in a different way. I really want you to empower yourself to approach your social media with a commitment to your authenticity because that's where your value lies. Without committing to your authenticity in social media, you will cause yourself stress and send yourself a harmful message that you're not enough. Social media can be a very weird place that can leave you feeling terrible, so you really have to lovingly commit to yourself to have a real and very smart perspective. When you shut off your phone or close your computer, you deserve to think you are enough. Up until now, you may have thought other people's likes are most important to making you feel good, but it's *your* like and love that will always make you feel the best.

I want to share something with you that I've always tried to teach my girls. You have to value who you are and not portray yourself on social media as something you're not. You also have to value yourself enough to not be portrayed on social media as something you're not. I know those both sort of sound like the same advice, but they're not.

Here's what I mean by the first part: don't post things about yourself that seem or look like something that isn't authentically you just because social media can be a place of performance. I understand that you may feel you have to present a perfect image of yourself. If you fall into the trap where you're posting "perfect image" pictures of yourself just for likes, it will end up leaving you feeling empty. It may give you instant gratification, but that doesn't last or fill you up. If you post things on social media that have been embellished, edited, and heavily filtered, there are not enough likes in the world to leave you feeling authentic with yourself. You'll be sending yourself a message that you and your life aren't good enough to present authentically. That may seem dramatic, but that pattern really can hurt your self-esteem.

Of course no one is up for posting gross, unattractive, or boring pictures of him- or herself. I'm not saying you need to do that, because that's not authentic either, but I encourage you to "be" rather than "seem." Be who you are, rather than trying to seem like something else. Don't fall prey to thinking you have to seem so perfect—or else little by little, you'll eat away at your confidence without you even understanding how. Being always feels better than seeming! Being authentic to please yourself is what gets you comfortable in your own skin. There is beauty and power in *being* who you really are!

Authentically expressing yourself feels so much better than launching a superficial picture or message. Try concentrating more on the experience or the place where you took the photograph. Be authentic by sharing a piece of your life and a piece of you so people can authentically get to know you as a person. You're not just a pretty face, right? No one cares about what you post more than you do, so empower yourself to want to make you proud.

The other meaning of "Don't post anything that doesn't portray the real you" is this: you are working hard on yourself. You are growing your values and your pride in yourself. Make sure your post or someone else's post of you doesn't set you up for judgment where people can make false and negative assumptions about you. Value yourself. Take charge of your reputation, and if your authentic self desires and deserves respect, don't fall prey to any social media posts that suggest something different about you. You are respectable, so make sure the post reflects that.

There are posts that get girls attention—but attention is not respect. Attention is momentary and doesn't always mean something that is positive or feels good later. Respect is solid and always feels good. Respect is greater than attention. Self-respect will bring you confidence and joy and will lead you to a meaningful life and meaningful relationships.

If you're authentic in what you post, you will respect yourself for it. You can also figure out who authentically cares about you and not a faked perfect image. Many people like images, but it's not really the person they are liking; it's the momentary image. We all want authentic people in our lives who authentically care about us. Next time you post, I hope you'll empower yourself to make sure it really feels authentic to you and shows proper respect to you.

One last thing I hope you'll think about in regard to authenticity and social media. When you're participating, please understand that being authentic doesn't mean lacking privacy or feeling obligated to give out private details of every aspect of your life. It's important to your well-being to hold back parts of you and your life for yourself, your privacy, and the people you're closest to. That doesn't mean you're hiding you or being inauthentic; it's just that not everyone is entitled to all parts of you, whether on social media or in life in general. It's not healthy to have everything set on "public," so set some of yourself and your life on "friends only" and "only me." You don't need the world's constant feedback on you; it's too confusing. Share what feels safe, authentic, and right to you. Have dignity, and be proud of what you're authentically saying.

There are many pieces of your life, and there will be even more pieces to it as you grow. You will find more peace when there is authenticity within those pieces. Empower yourself to keep growing in authenticity—the way you look; the way you express your thoughts, feelings, values, and beliefs; the way you behave; the way you do relationships; the work you do; the things you choose to do with your time; the accomplishments you chase; the way you interact with people; the way you do anything. Authenticity will leave you feeling authentically beautiful and authentically strong and powerful.

Authenticity is beautiful. Authenticity feels beautiful.

Grow yourself beautiful.

Four

The most beautiful and powerful women in the world know who they are and what they value so they can follow their hearts.

Grow Yourself B-E-A-**U**-T-I-F-U-L
U Is for Unplugging
Getting to Know Yourself Is Beautiful

You are growing up in a world where technology is a huge part of your life. You use technology for school and work and also for play and as a way to decompress. You are plugged into smartphones, tablets, computers, watches, and so on, all sending you messages all day long. I know a part of you even feels scared at the thought of disconnecting from any of those devices for fear you may miss something!

Have you ever used your computer and it was "glitchy" that day, just not functioning well, maybe even hot to the touch like it needed a break? So you shut it down and maybe even unplugged it for a bit. When you plugged it back in and turned it on, it began to reboot. It was refreshed and ran stronger and more efficiently. Well, think of yourself much the same way here. Anytime you're plugged in, you have many messages coming at you. It's easy to feel glitchy, overheated, and spinning from being plugged in so often and for so long.

When you don't really *need* to stay plugged in for school or work, I want you to consider stealing some of your time away from technology and giving it to yourself. Would you ever consider getting rid of some of the unneeded technology time and giving it to your personal growth, restoration, and well-being?

I want to help you understand the importance of shifting focus from being plugged into the technology world 24/7 and living with FOMO (fear of missing out) to protecting yourself more and allowing yourself to miss some things in order to gain a lot. I want to help you understand the value of unplugging yourself from the noise of the rest of the world and how important that is to your mental health. After reading this chapter, I hope you'll empower yourself to take unplugged time and devote that time to yourself, because it's essential to your positive growth as a living, breathing human being with needs.

You are the most important relationship you will ever have. The relationship you have with you is the one that matters most. You're the one you will always spend the most time with. No one will ever be able to take care of you and love you like you can. Only you can really understand your needs—what it takes to fill you up or know when you are overloaded. It is so important to your health and your relationships with yourself and others that you take time to unplug. That relationship with yourself depends on having time with yourself where your devices don't get to be part of it. Investing more of your time in yourself will nurture you and help you grow. You deserve special time with yourself to build your foundation, feel centered, and get calmly focused.

When you are plugged in, you are receiving other people's information and their energy. If it's good energy, hey, that's great! That's the bright side. However, when there is a lot going on in the world or within someone, if the world or the person sends out negative energy, you're allowing yourself to be a sponge of it each time you "plug in." I want you to begin to think about how important it is to start protecting your energy so you don't get overwhelmed and start spinning.

Another very important thing to give thought to is if you spend a lot of your time plugged into your devices, you're often missing out on something real and alive right in front of you that's a pulsing part of your life!

As humans, we are made to need the "real." Does your world that you create with your time allow you to see, smell, taste, feel, and touch life in person? You are designed to get soulful fulfillment by engaging all your senses. When you deprive yourself of real life, it will make you feel like something is missing. Have you ever felt that? You may not even understand why you feel undernourished, lonely, or depressed sometimes, but it's because you're missing the real that a human craves. When you are engaging in real life, you'll really understand exactly what I mean. You will feel nourishment you've been missing.

Our phones have become attached to us. They give us instant access to the world, but they also give the world instant access to us. Some people are so addicted to their devices they feel the need to share their thoughts, concerns, or experiences to us all throughout the day via texts and phone calls and social media. Even when you're not on your phone, if you have it next to you, you're basically still plugged in. It's understandable that sometimes you have to be able to be reached for various reasons, but when it's not necessary, you deserve to silence it and go unplugged—then just check back on it as your responsibilities dictate. You can then decide when you want to interrupt you. You have to have uninterrupted time to get to know yourself, build yourself, and build your world and your life. You have to have uninterrupted time in order to feel relaxed and centered. If you can do this for yourself, you will begin to feel the power and beauty of being unplugged. Your peace and joy are tied to that!

Of course, I understand that our computers and tablets have also become so important because that's where we work, play, listen to music, watch videos or Netflix, and so on. But we can't smell, talk to, or touch life when we're on them. It might be interesting to you to keep a log of how much time you spend plugged in and how much time you spend feeling, tasting, smelling, hearing, or touching something around you. How much time do you spend talking directly with a living, breathing human? If you aren't plugged into real life, you will feel stress, depression, and isolation. I hope you will regularly remind yourself that humans need to be humans. Unplug and tap into your senses to really be a human and connect like a human needs to. That might seem silly, but if you try it, you will want to make it more of your way of life. If you have felt something is missing in your life, unplug! Baby steps if you need to—but unplug!

Even if we think we are unplugging from working or learning on our devices to go on social media for our fun, we still aren't using our time to reboot, replenish, and build ourselves. Using social media to decompress from responsibilities is fun and healthy only if you are really plugged into your life when you're not on it. Being social and feeling connected to other people, as I mentioned, is a necessary part of human life. But when it comes to social media, seeing what other people are up to will only be fun if you feel you are in charge of your own life and you like what you're doing with it. If you don't feel heavily invested in your own real life, social media can create jealous, inadequate, lonely, isolated, and drained feelings.

The only way to feel like you are in charge of your life and what you're doing with your time is to unplug and then use that time being human, resting, and growing yourself in enjoyable, meaningful ways. Unplugging will give you the fair time to ask yourself, "What do I want my life to look like? What are my dreams? What do I love? How do I feel about different things going on with me and with my life? What are my values?" Unplugging will give you time to pray, meditate, dream, restore, self-reflect, build, be, and do.

You can't grow yourself strong and interesting and beautiful if you're devoted more to an electronic device than to yourself. You can't grow yourself strong, interesting, and beautiful if you are only a spectator of someone else's life on television, Facebook, Twitter, Instagram, Snapchat, and so on. Empower yourself to grow your life and participate in life rather than spend too much using an electronic device or watching other people's lives on them. You have to plug into what's right for you and right in front of you!

Your life should feel the most interesting, entertaining, and meaningful to you. If you take this important time to regularly unplug, you will give yourself time to rest, reboot, imagine, dream, try, learn, and grow in ways that will feel good to you and make you proud of yourself and your life! It's in that time that you will find yourself and build yourself. You will feel so powerful and beautiful after you've unplugged.

Unplugging to spend time with yourself to get to know yourself and grow yourself is beautiful. Grow yourself beautiful!

WAYS TO GROW WHILE YOU'RE UNPLUGGED

- Engage in self-care.
- Pray.
- Rest.
- Sleep!
- Meditate.
- Write your feelings and plans in a journal.
- Write down your values.
- Breathe deeply and fully.

- Spend quality time with yourself to hear your own deep feelings.
- Ask yourself what interests you.
- Hope.
- Imagine.
- Dream.
- Do something out of your comfort zone.
- Get in touch with your gratitude for all that is right in your world.
- Invest in your health and fitness.
- Coexist closely and quietly with someone you enjoy being around.
- Reach out to someone you want to get to know more.
- Have a meaningful conversation and bond with someone you care about.
- Touch, taste, smell, and feel the life around you!
- Educate yourself on anything for school.
- Educate yourself on some kind of work you want to do.
- Educate yourself on something fun that excites you.
- Develop a hobby.
- Create something—make food, or make art!
- Do something meaningful to you.
- Plan something fun.
- Do something that feeds your soul.
- Sing, listen to music, make music, or dance.
- Read something not on a device.
- Write or send a note to connect with someone.
- Go outside and take in nature.
- Spend some time with animals.
- Take beautiful and artsy photographs.
- Volunteer.
- Love.

What else can you think of to do while you're unplugged to help yourself grow?

Five

The most beautiful and powerful women in the world live with thankfulness and gratitude.

Grow Yourself B-E-A-U-**T**-I-F-U-L
T Is for Thankfulness and Gratefulness
Living with Thanks and Gratitude Is Beautiful

You've probably heard the expression an "attitude of gratitude." Well, what does that really mean, and how do we know if we have it? You may even ask yourself, "Is it even relevant to me?" You also may wonder whether this is something you have to be born with or if it's something you can cultivate. I don't know if I can answer if you were born with it, but I strongly believe it's something you can cultivate. It's a mindset that can cultivate a heart set! It's a heart set that can help you feel happy and content. It's a heart set that brings you even more things to be grateful for—followed by deeper joy.

Let's explore this attitude of gratitude thing together, and let's begin with the good ole example of "Is the glass of water half-full or half-empty?" Do you know where you stand on this observation? When you look at a glass filled halfway with water, what do you see? Do you see and think of it as half-full or half-empty? Take a moment to think about that and see where you land.

If you think of it as half-full, you are definitely on the right track for an attitude of gratitude. If you automatically notice the glass is half-empty, you may be someone who quickly goes to thinking about what you don't have, as opposed to what you do. When you become aware of all that is present for you and about you, then you really get to feel the depth of what you do have and appreciate it. Deep fulfillment, contentment, and joy follow appreciation.

When you begin to really cultivate an attitude of gratitude, you can take your observations and feeling of gratitude to an even deeper level. You can then not only see a glass that is half-full but also feel very optimistic that you will always have water because you see you have a glass as well. And when you have a glass, you can keep refilling it with more water, right?!

When you can shift focus to see what *is* there rather than what isn't, your mind and heart can go to gratitude so much more quickly, relieving stress. You will worry much less about water missing in half the glass. Developing and living with an attitude of gratitude is all about becoming aware of and concentrating on what you have, rather than what you don't—and being thankful for it.

When we feel thankful, we feel more security and joy, and it cultivates positive energy within us! That positive energy brings us a gracious heart and attitude that even make others want to be around us and help us too. Having a gracious attitude actually makes people want to help you fill up "your glass"! People like being around and helping gracious people.

I want to help you grow yourself with a thankful mindset. Conditioning the way you look at what you already are and what you already have will help you identify how many blessings you have in ways you never thought or felt before. When things are going right, it will magnify your joy and happiness. If you can learn how to be thankful even during life storms, you will be able to cope more easily and comfortably—with a sense of joy.

Thankful and *grateful* make up this mindset and perspective—two different words but very intertwined. They go hand in hand, especially when we're talking about growing ourselves in a way in which we make them virtues of our being and practices of how we live.

Merriam-Webster's official definition of the word *thankful* references being "conscious of benefit received." That's such a perfectly simple way for us to understand the word and approach. *Thankful* means being conscious and aware of what you are receiving in your life.

So first, you challenge yourself to become more aware and more conscious. You can really grow yourself by becoming more conscious and aware of your personal gifts and life blessings and the benefits you receive because of them. As you practice this attitude, you will feel more deeply thankful through all your positive moments. This mindset automatically brings you more joy because you uncover the specialness of you and your life. As you really, really cultivate this mindset and attitude, you will find many treasures to be thankful for, even in your toughest, roughest, darkest experiences.

Now for *grateful*. Merriam-Webster's definition of *grateful* describes it as "pleasing by reason of comfort supplied or discomfort alleviated." Wow! This is perfect. The definition describes exactly why I want this as a way of life for you. If you are grateful, you can supply yourself with comfort. And yes, you really can alleviate discomfort for yourself by being grateful. If becoming more aware of your beautiful personal gifts as a human and the gifts you have in your life—and then growing in your gratitude for those things—can really bring you comfort and alleviate stress, then oh my goodness, yes, let's help you grow in being thankful and grateful! What powerful tools for yourself!

I hope you can understand the lens you choose to see your life through can deeply affect you. I hope you will empower yourself to shift your lens and focus to feeling thankful and grateful. I want you to do that for yourself because I know from experience it's a magical formula. I know it really can make your life easier and more joyful. It has helped me so much in life. By having awareness of all that I've been blessed with and feeling grateful for it, I have found joy even during my roughest and darkest times. I want that for you. You deserve to have more comfort and joy on your journey of life, and this is a way to have that.

In addition to your own life experiences, you will go through many ups and downs just because of the various people you'll love in your life. You will have many different roles, such as daughter, sister, friend, student, employee, wife, mom—the list goes on. When you have different roles and many people and experiences in your life, you are guaranteed to have troubles, worries, sorrows, obstacles, and illnesses. That's okay. It's all part of what's called a *full life*. Don't let that make you afraid of a full life. A full life is a great thing! However, with a full life, we are guaranteed challenges and struggles ... and some dark times.

The good news is that intertwined with that reality of bumps, a full life brings us far more joys than a not-full life does. So let's not shy away from a full life; let's help you develop tools to be able to enjoy it to the fullest. Our lives are purposely designed for both joys and troubles. It's the combination that makes life great! I hope knowing that you will never be the only one tasked with having to go through hard times brings you comfort in itself. In spite of the hard things we'll all go through, the more we grow ourselves to cope, the more comfortable, joyful, and rich our life's journey can become. You can actually learn how to still feel the joys during life's bumps and struggles. Thankfulness and gratitude play a gigantic role in coping with these bumps.

Do you feel that you already have an attitude of gratitude? Do you feel you have that perspective? If someone had asked me that when I was a young woman, I don't know how I would have answered. I've only become aware I have this attitude as I have gone through my life. As I had similar tough circumstances to some of my friends, I learned I have a gratitude for life that I didn't know I had. I saw some of my friends fall into very dark places and let grief and disappointments take the spotlight of their lives for very long periods of time. When I didn't stay low as long as they did, even when some of the exact same things happened to me, I began to wonder why. I know I'm a sensitive person. In fact, sometimes I think I'm too sensitive. So as a sensitive, deeply feeling person, it puzzled me why I didn't stay low and stuck as long while I faced the same types of hard situations as some of my friends. Was there something wrong with me? I certainly understood and felt the seriousness of the situations. So why wasn't I as dark, and as dark for so long, as some of them?

I have thought a lot about that over the years, searching for why I'm able to move more quickly through some of these hardships. Thankfulness and gratitude were my answer. I realized I live with an attitude of gratitude. I realized a pattern not just with me but also with others who live with deep gratitude. I certainly didn't know enough to seek out this attitude, but I know I'm glad I have it—even if I developed it by accident. I hope you feel that your life is a beautiful gift. I hope you will want to live it as pleasurably and joyfully as possible. It's no fun to live in the dark. You don't have to stay stuck in the dark. We can't control a lot of the dark things that will happen to us. And identifying all the light in our lives allows the light to sustain us during dark times. If we can shift more focus on all the beautiful light in our lives, there is no way the darkness can trap us in. Dark times are inevitable, but you really can teach yourself to be grateful for those times too. They teach us so much about life and ourselves. After we show ourselves we can get past those dark times, we are able to live with even deeper joy and bigger gratitude. We feel beautiful and powerful when we know how to get through the dark!

I want you to learn to see all the light and things that are going right in your world. However, for the purpose of grasping and developing this concept, I want you to take time to think about all parts of your life. Just for a few moments right now, think about anything causing you stress, sadness, loneliness, anxiety, or depression. I hope you haven't had to lose someone you love yet, but maybe you are having to deal with the loss of someone important right now. Maybe you're having some physical health issues. Maybe you are dealing with mental illness. Maybe you have someone you love who is dealing with an illness. Maybe you don't feel as significant as you wish to feel. Maybe you don't feel as loved as you need to be. Maybe you're in a tough circumstance or being bullied or mistreated right now. Maybe you feel troubled by all the craziness going on in the world right now. Maybe you've had some bad grades lately. Whatever it might be, because you're human, I know you have things in your life right now that are upsetting you. Take time to think about what is feeling dark to you. I think it's very important to be honest with yourself and acknowledge all the feelings that come with any of these tough life circumstances.

As you think about your life circumstances and challenges, I wonder if you can find anything about a tough circumstance that is helping you grow. Is anything about it bringing something good into your life? Is it bringing you closer to someone or people you love? Has it shown you that you are tougher than you thought? Has it taught you how to care for yourself better? Has it made you love the normal you that you had in your life before it? Has it shown you that you have people in your life who have your back and want to help you? Think about the situation, and see if there is anything you can be grateful for about that dark circumstance.

Let's now have you think about all the positive things in your life. I left you some journaling pages at the back of this book if you'd like to write these down. What are your gifts as a person? What do you like about yourself? What do you like about the people in your life? What are the gifts of your life? What about you and your life makes you feel lucky? Those are your lights! Those are things to be grateful for, and by becoming aware of them, concentrating on them, and thanking them, you can get past the dark. That's how you develop your mindset and attitude of being thankful and grateful.

Because I have lived and watched the power of positivity and felt the joy that comes from thankfulness and gratitude, I know this is something that can really help you and make your journey easier. I really hope you empower yourself to shift more focus to this as a way of life so you can learn how to alleviate stress. By living with your heart in a more thankful mode, you can really increase your happiness, health, and well-being.

Each and every day, if you can look at your day and your life and all the positive blessings you have and live gratefully, you will watch your light and blessings multiply and *feel* your joy and comfort multiply. You will have less time and less desire to look for what you don't have or compare yourself and your life to other people and their lives. You will fall so in love with what's going right you won't want to stress by overanalyzing and being overly critical of yourself, your life, or others. Being thankful will raise your confidence and self-esteem too. Gratitude will make you feel stronger and more beautiful.

In your everyday life, if you can resist locking in on troubles and focusing on loss and what you don't have, and begin to look at all the things that are going right for you and all the beautiful things you already are, you can positively raise the vibrational frequency of your self-love and your life!

You can grow yourself with this beautiful, strong, and thankful quality. You can be the one who lifts up yourself in times of trouble and be the one who does that for others too. When you are going through a hard time, you can remind yourself that you're grateful by becoming aware of the whole experience.

You will still have times when you struggle to feel positive and capable That's okay. Life can be very hard, and we'll never handle it perfectly. So build a circle of friends who share your thankful attitude. Those friends will share their thankful hearts and spirits and can help lift you up when you need that help. Together, you can make a hard time just a passing time rather than a way of life. We suddenly feel a lot more positive and hopeful about our day and our life when we have a circle of friends around us who share our thankful attitude. Building that takes time, so have patience. Staying positive will make that happen sooner for you.

Next time you go through a tough time, interrupt your anxiety with gratitude toward the situation! Rather than falling deep into the experience, making you anxious, depressed, or bitter, remind yourself you can live better if you receive the bad time, meaningful messages, and personal growth with a thankful heart. I know it will seem hard, but each time you get through something, you can then remind yourself of that tough time you had and how it made you a better, smarter, more resilient person—so be grateful for that experience. Approach your new trials with gratitude, and it'll surprise you how you steal their power and move through them more quickly and with powerful meaning.

As you try to grow with this practice and perspective, it helps to tap deeper into your spiritual side. What I mean by that is tap into the beautiful things that affect your human spirit. You will need to gently encourage yourself through this process. To get this started right away, each night when you slip into bed, reach deep into your soul, and start feeling and thanking everything that went right that day, beginning with being able to wake up alive and in a clean, warm, comfortable bed, and go from there. You will learn that you can immediately calm yourself as you call out with gratitude for so many things you once took for granted.

There are so many wonderful and positive things about you and your life that really are very special. Each day, you can grow stronger by taking a positive inventory of yourself, your moments, your day, and your life.

Let me throw you some maybes about your world just to help you get your thoughts started and your attitude of gratitude cranked up. These maybes will either hit home or help you stimulate your mind, heart, and soul toward some of your gifts.

Maybe you are a great friend and no one else you know listens to and supports others quite the way you do. People can be very self-focused, so what a special gift if you possess that! Make a list of some of your personal gifts that you bring to people in your life.

Maybe you have a family member or a friend you can trust with all your feelings who you know will be there for you and love you no matter what. How wonderful, because there are many people who feel all alone. Who are the people in your life you can trust and count on?

Maybe you smelled fresh-baked cookies today. What is it about that smell that warms our hearts and gives us comfort? What smells bring comfort and joy to you?

Maybe you have a coach or teacher who just seems to get you. There are so many people who feel misunderstood. Do you have that someone who understands you?

Maybe you are blessed with a heart that is more tender than the hearts of many people you know. People like you are a gift to the world! Think about that for a moment; is your heart one of the tender and beautiful ones that make our world a better place?

Maybe you can hear a sound right now that gives you comfort and a feeling of safety in your home. There are people who have to try to sleep while listening to violence, unrest, or street noise. Do you get to experience a quiet home or a quiet place where you can feel safe and relaxed?

Maybe you ran a mile today and never thought that was something you could do with your body. Are you able to do physical exercise that makes you feel proud and strong?

Maybe you went to the doctor for a checkup and were told you are very healthy. If we have health, then we get to have life! Do you feel gratitude for your health?

Maybe you're not healthy right now but you're lucky enough to have people or resources that are helping you get better. Who are the people in your life who care about your health and well-being? Who are the people you trust to help you through it?

Maybe you had a good cry today that left you feeling in touch with your emotions and cleansed. Being able to feel and sort through your feelings is beautiful. When was the last time you had a good cry? Do you feel grateful that you have the ability to feel?

Maybe you had a great deep laugh today. Laughter is such a great stress reliever and reminder of all that is good. What makes you laugh? Do you have anyone in your life who makes you laugh? Do you possess the gift of lifting others and making them laugh?

Maybe you saw something beautiful outside today because you have the ability to see. What do you see every day that adds beauty to your world? Make a list of people, places, or things that are beautiful in your eyes and fill your soul.

Maybe you smelled your clothes and they smelled so clean it almost made you cry for people who don't have clean clothes. What important things have you taken for granted that you wish all people could have too?

Maybe you felt thirsty and were able to get safe water by just turning on your sink. Have you ever thought of that to be a privilege and convenience for you? Maybe you were able to get your favorite coffee or tea drink and didn't even have to get out of the car to get it? Is this a convenience and comfort you get to experience?

Maybe you tasted something amazing today that lit up your taste buds, body, and life. What foods make you love life?

Maybe you have a pet that just wants to be near you because you make each other feel so loved. Have you ever experienced love for and from an animal?

Maybe you resolved a conflict or situation that has been weighing heavily on your mind. Take a moment, and think about that. Do you feel grateful and proud you got through it?

Maybe you were able to help someone today. When someone needs you, do you feel grateful you are someone who can help others?

Maybe you learned something today that made you realize you're smarter than you thought. How does being smart make you feel?

Maybe you heard your favorite song or heard a song for the first time today that made you feel something beautiful. Do you have songs and artists that help you get through life?

Maybe you're one of the nicest, kindest girls on your campus. Do you know how many people need you to touch their life?

Maybe nothing went wrong today. How often can you say that? Have you ever thanked a day because nothing went wrong? If you took note of these days, I wonder if it'd surprised you how many there are!

I've left you a few pages at the end of this book to use as the beginning of a gratitude practice. Think of those pages as a mini gratitude journal, and try taking a few moments a day to start writing down all the things you're grateful for. Writing those down will help you become more aware of them. And on days when you don't feel quite as grateful, read through your grateful pages, which I believe will bring you comfort. It will help you refocus yourself in a positive, more joyful, less stressful direction.

Every time you become aware of something in you or your life that's good, the anxiety train will get derailed because gratitude can keep you centered and calm and on track.

As you grow in your thankfulness, you will grow tremendously in your strength. You will be able to look at all experiences, good and bad, with thankful eyes and a grateful heart!

People who live with gratitude are strong and beautiful, shine bright, and relax more through life. People who live with gratitude can comfort themselves and those around them. Thankfulness is a grounding and beautiful quality.

Grow yourself more thankful. Grow yourself in gratitude.

Grow yourself beautiful!

Six

The most beautiful and powerful
women in the world are resilient.

Grow Yourself B-E-A-U-T-I-F-U-L
I Is for "I Am Resilient"
Resilience Is Beautiful

Did you know you can grow yourself to be more resilient? Did you know you can actually teach yourself to recover quicker and stronger after you've had something bad happen? I want to help you grow yourself stronger and more resilient. I want you to develop your resilience so you feel assured that you are someone who knows how to get back up when you get knocked down!

As we go through some of these life struggles, disappointments, twists, and turns, I think one of the things that causes us the most stress is not being sure of what or how much we're capable of handling. As you've been growing up, society sent your generation the message of "everyone gets a trophy." You didn't have to be the best, you didn't have to win, but you were still going to get a trophy because someone thought it would hurt your feelings or you couldn't handle it if you didn't. That was a really unfair message sent to you.

Speaking metaphorically, you shouldn't get a trophy if you didn't really earn it. I don't know how that makes you feel, but I sincerely believe that you probably don't want a trophy you feel you didn't honestly earn. I also believe that you are strong enough to handle not getting one. The people sending you that message had good intentions, but it undermined your ability to handle and cope with the truth. You are capable of earning your own trophies, and you are capable of coping when you aren't good enough at something to get one. You are not a fragile snowflake. I know you can handle life's truths. You will empower yourself to keep growing and become stronger, more capable, and more resilient—because you are going to have to handle life's truths.

We don't all have to be good at everything, and we are all really good at some things. Some people will excel in sports, some in the classroom, some at work, some on the stage, some in the art studio, some with in the community, and so on. It takes awhile for us to figure out where we will earn our trophies, but I promise you, you have talents, gifts, and strengths that will be trophy worthy! When you build your resilience, that's one of the biggest trophies you can ever earn in life, because if you're resilient, you're winning at life!

I've made an observation as a mother as I've raised my girls. Many parents out there accidentally send messages to their kids that they are not resilient. As a mom, I understand firsthand how much we want to protect you, our kids, from any hurt or disappointment. As parents, it means so much to us to protect you from that feeling that you aren't good enough at something or that someone doesn't like you. However, that feeling like you're not good enough can be temporary if you empower yourself to keep moving forward so you can find your people, talents, powers, and successes! Resilience keeps you moving forward!

Real life doesn't allow us, as your parents, to follow you around forever, smoothing the road ahead for you and making sure you won't feel struggles, disappointment, or hurt. We would if we could, but that isn't reality, and besides, I've learned you really don't need us to do that for you. You are stronger and more capable than you even know. What we need to do for you is let you empower yourself to see that you will be just fine. We need to empower you to build your resilience.

You're human, so you will make mistakes. You will disappoint yourself and people you love. You will be hurt by people, sometimes even your family members or best friends. You will be treated unfairly, maybe even by someone you admire. You will not be good at everything, and that's okay; no one is. You won't keep getting trophies you don't really deserve, and you may not even get a trophy when you really do deserve one, but you will be fine. I promise you will show yourself that you will be fine. Not only will you be fine, you will learn there's still joy among your struggles. That will build you. Each time you are struggling, disappointed, or hurt, you become stronger and more resilient. Resilience is like a muscle. You will keep building it each time you use it. Going through hard times will not break you; it will build you, and it will make you stronger! You are growing yourself as a resilient person!

Growing from the "everyone gets a trophy" period of your younger life to the realization that many people in your older life couldn't actually care less about you ever getting a trophy can feel painful at first. Most people are too busy chasing their own trophies to care whether you get one. It's hard to grow from the coddling stage of people worrying about you having a trophy so you feel good to the stage of your life where you feel abandoned by that philosophy and feel people are busy worrying way too much about themselves. That reality can really overwhelm you, leaving you feeling abandoned at times. It doesn't have to, though, if you realize that part is not about you; it's about them chasing what they need. That's okay; you don't need them to present you with a trophy. You'll bring yourself what you need. You are capable of bringing in your own trophies!

Empower yourself to make your life about growing you, and let's not worry about why other people suddenly don't care about giving you trophies and praise. They are focusing on themselves, and you are going to focus on you—growing you in ways that make you so proud of yourself!

Our lives are supposed to have ups and downs. That's how we learn about ourselves, that's how we develop compassion for others, and that's how we learn to really love and appreciate life.

You'll be okay if your best friend finds a new one. You'll be okay if you get excluded. You'll be okay if someone makes fun of you. You'll be okay if someone else doesn't know your worth. You'll be okay if you make mistakes. You'll be okay if you don't make a team you wanted to make. You'll be okay if you make the team but the coaches never let you off the bench. You'll be okay if you aren't the size you want to be. You'll be okay if you don't get straight As. You'll be okay if you don't get your first choice in situations. You'll be okay if the boy you like doesn't like you. You'll be okay if you lose someone you love. You'll be okay if your life plans get changed. You'll be okay if you are struggling. You'll be okay if you have anxiety or depression. Whatever your struggle, you will be okay. You are growing in your resilience to handle it and get through it—that's how you know you will be okay.

Part of being okay is showing yourself you know when to ask for help when you need it. Ask for help from the people you love. Ask them to hold your hand while you grow in your strength and resilience. If you feel there isn't a hand available, that's when you dig deep and be there for yourself. Reach for yours—it's strong, and it's always there! Yours is the strongest hand you'll ever know. It's the only hand that really knows what you need. It will take time to figure that out and believe in it. You're growing your hand in a way, which will be your favorite anyway—because it's the one you can be assured is always there!

Here's something important I hope will comfort you and I want you to hang on to so you won't feel alone with your struggles. Everything and anything you feel, many, many girls feel it too. I have been around a lot of girls for twenty-five years, and most of you have the same struggles. People are just good at hiding their struggles. You're not weird. You're not weak. You are human. You have struggles. You are not the only one who has struggles. You have feelings about your struggles. You should allow yourself to feel. It's good to feel your feelings. Other people have these feelings too. Feelings are how you know you are a loving human being and that you're alive! It really is okay to feel all those feelings that come with your disappointment and struggles. Be proud that you are someone who feels. Be proud that you are someone who uses your feelings to build you! Be proud that you are someone who can get back on your feet! Be proud that you are someone who can bring yourself through darkness back to the light! Be proud that you are building your resilience. Be proud that you are earning that trophy of resilience.

If it doesn't rain, we don't appreciate the sunshine. If we don't fall, we don't learn how strong we are once we get back up. If we don't lose, we never get to appreciate how good it feels to win. If we're never sick, we never appreciate how wonderful it is being healthy and alive. If we don't spend time in the dark, we never know how good the light feels. If we don't struggle, we can never understand how much other people need our compassion.

It's okay to have these periods of hurt, angst, struggles, and disappointments; you'll be fine. You're growing stronger every minute, every hour, and every single day! How do you know you'll be fine? Because starting today, when things go wrong, you are going to start pointing out to yourself how you grew from other times that seemed terrible. Remember how you got back up and moved forward? You are going to start looking at struggles as opportunities to grow your resilience. Resilience will give you confidence in yourself and help you feel more in control of your destiny! Resilience will make you feel strong and beautiful!

Let's go back to thankfulness and gratitude for a moment. Each time you have a struggle, thank it! It's making you a badass! Taking time to thank a problem forces you to take an inventory of how it made you better. The struggle is what makes you more resilient. I truly believe the biggest trophy that can ever be earned in life is the one for resilience. That's the trophy you'll be proudest of. That will be your trophy that keeps you moving forward. It will show you your ability to handle problems and to keep growing in life. It will show you how to live with joy!

I had a saying with my girls when they were faced with an uphill battle or tough time. I always told them, "Don't try to go around it, over it, or under it—you have to go through it, and you can do it. It's only when you go through it that you can really deal with it, conquer it, and get it behind you." When you have that struggle or uphill battle, be brave, face it head-on, and go through it. You can handle it.

You can handle these battles by building your resilience in many ways. Start by empowering yourself to remember all your personal positives and life's positives. Also, search for any positives that may be in the situation or that may result from the situation. Focus on the positive ahead because the negative feelings that come from the struggles and tough times are usually temporary. Your resilience can make those feelings temporary!

To have resilience, you have to take good care of yourself. We'll cover this more in the self-care chapter, but caring for yourself in ways to keep you physically, mentally, and spiritually healthy is very important to being resilient. If you are well rested, centered, and strong, you will have more control of your stress level and how you choose to respond to tough situations.

You can build your resilience by focusing on solutions rather than staying focused on the problem. Be determined to not stay stuck; try to develop creative solutions that will move you past it. If a solution will take time, think of creative small steps toward it. Just creatively analyzing it, making an action plan, and executing it will take your focus off the worry. It will give you a break and the confidence that you will get through it.

Not staying stuck is very important to building your resilience—and resilience is very important to not staying stuck. Be willing to accept that maybe things won't always go just the way you planned. Be open to considering that a problem may have interrupted your plans to bring you something better or to make you better. Be flexible, and don't allow yourself to stay stuck in what cannot be. The more times you "unstick" yourself from what cannot be, the more you grow in your resilience.

A sense of humor is also so important to building your resilience. Even if just for a few minutes, if you can find reasons to laugh in a tough situation, you can diminish your troubled feelings and alleviate some of your stress. It will help refresh you and allow you to handle the problem better. Laughter is beautiful medicine. It can instantly make you feel better! Don't forget to laugh at yourself sometimes too. If you find yourself being a drama queen over the smaller stuff, have a giggle at yourself, and remind yourself to calm down. The bigger the deal you make out your problems, the bigger they will always feel to you.

Keep building loving connections with friends and family. Include people you love and trust in your problems when it's safe. Having those connections can assist with your resilience because that love and support will help you feel less affected by things that go wrong or tough situations. Your loving circle of people can also help remind you of all your strengths and gifts when you are low and forget to focus on them.

Whatever comes your way—no matter how big or how dark—after you've handled it, it loses its power! You don't have to let it define you, or keep living it over and over again.

Go through it—not around it, under it, or over it! Be brave. You can do it. You'll be fine. I know those struggles can make you feel so broken at the time. But when you find your life lessons and silver linings from them and keep getting up and keep trying, that is being resilient. That is a champion! That's trophy worthy!

Being brave, being strong, and refusing to be a victim of any circumstance will make you grow in such a beautifully strong and resilient way. You will develop incredible self-love and self-confidence. You will feel so proud of yourself. You're going to feel so much more in control when your life has those twists, turns, struggles, and disappointments.

Because you are growing your confidence and handling tough times, you will feel more joy in your journey of life. You are growing yourself in a way that makes you no longer dependent on other people telling you you'll be fine; you'll see firsthand how resilient you are and how far you've come. You will be able to assure yourself that you'll be fine. Each and every time you get knocked down, you'll learn you have the ability to recover and get back up. You are also growing yourself in many other areas. The more physically and mentally healthy you become through the self-care, self-love, and self-confidence you're developing, the more resilient you will be! Every subject in every chapter of this book will help you grow in your resilience.

Empower yourself to grow in your resilience. Resilience is comforting, strong, and beautiful.

Grow yourself beautiful.

Seven

The most beautiful and powerful women
in the world live with faith and hope.

Grow Yourself B-E-A-U-T-I-**F**-U-L
F Is for Faith
Living with Faith and Hope Is Beautiful

> But when I am afraid, I will put my trust in you.
> —Psalm 56:3 (NLT)

Faith is a very personal subject. Whether or not someone believes in God or practices a religion, it is a very personal subject and experience. Everyone is on his or her own personal journey of faith, and that should be respected. I personally have never liked it when someone tries to push beliefs on me or convince me that my faith should look a certain way or that I have to worship God or something else in a particular way. No matter if you believe in God with a strong faith, you believe in him with an underlying faith, you're unsure he exists at all, or you have faith in another power different from God, I hope you will still read this chapter with an open heart. That is because if you have ever felt that you need someone or some greater power than your own to help you and lift your worries, this could be a really important chapter for you—important not because I want to force my belief in God on you but because I don't want you to ever feel alone.

As I said, I believe someone's faith—and what he or she does with it—is his or her own business. In fact, if I'm honest, I've had times in my life when I wasn't quite sure I actually had a personal relationship with God. I was brought up Catholic, and due to what my parents and church taught me, I definitely believed God existed, but I don't know that I really felt he knew me or served me personally. I think I always thought I was just supposed to serve him because, well, he is God. My faith was so embedded in me through Catholic teachings that I went through the motions and tried hard to live in ways I thought "served" the Lord, but in my younger days, never did it occur to me he was my friend and he would be there for me.

When I was twelve, much to my extremely painful surprise, my parents got divorced. I was very close to both my parents and loved what I *thought* was a solid family with my parents, my sister, and my brother. My mom and dad were great parents who loved us, but because of their circumstances at that time, a lot of their lives and attention focused on their personal lives and new partners. I didn't feel like it was on me. I often felt unexplainably lonely and longed for my home that had all my family under one roof and for that security and identity I once knew.

As some divorced kids do, I went back and forth between my mom's house and my dad's house in order to spend time with both of them. My dad's new wife had two kids from her previous marriage who began living with them. When I wanted time with my dad, we never had time alone, and it now included people I didn't really know at the time. When I visited my dad's house, to make matters worse, I felt like I was observing someone else's family using my dad. They didn't do it intentionally, but most stories at the dinner table involved all the things they all did together. When I went back to my home with my mom, I felt like I had left *my* dad in someone else's family, and my own house with my mom felt lonely without my whole family together and my dad's strong presence.

I didn't want to disappoint my good parents, who truly gave me a lot of love and were trying their best in this new situation, but I felt sad, misplaced, and lonely for some of my most formative years. I felt embarrassed to share these feelings with anyone, and like I said, I didn't want to hurt my parents' feelings because I knew how much they loved me even if everything seemed so different.

At the time, divorce was not as prevalent as it is now. In fact, my parents were really the first people I ever knew who got divorced, and I felt embarrassed and ashamed of it. I didn't really feel comfortable sharing my feelings with anyone, so I began to talk to the only person I thought I could talk to—me. At least that's who I thought I was talking to. My thoughts and talks to myself eventually became more like requests and prayers, and sooner or later, I realized I was talking to God, not myself. Maybe it was my Catholic upbringing that fell into place, or maybe he scooped me up and brought me close to him; that is the beautiful mystery of faith.

Up until that time, I don't know that I really understood I could talk to God like a trusted friend. I thought I was supposed to love him, but I didn't really know for sure he knew me and loved me. I didn't realize for a while that I had been talking to him all that time, because it wasn't like I got on my knees every time I shared my feelings and worries and wishes. He began serving me, instead of me serving him. I started realizing those talks were turning my feelings around, and many of my requests were being answered. I felt a sense of security that made the loneliness disappear when I realized there was a greater power with me. That power became real to me, and it helped me.

That was the first time I realized this was a relationship I could have. It wasn't one way at all. I started to look forward to praying at night—which actually became more like a conversation with a trusted friend. I then began to realize I could even talk to him for three seconds during the day when I just needed to feel I was around someone safe to talk to and I wouldn't hurt anyone's feelings or have someone judge me or my family. I received a fullness and comfort that I couldn't explain. I began to see hope every time I went to him for something during that hard time and then for many years to come.

I also have to admit, because I was young, I became selfish in the relationship. The relationship was often one-sided on my part because I would only go to him in times of stress or trouble. I often forgot to talk to him or thank him when everything was going well. From my youngest age I can remember to the age of twelve when my parents got divorced, I believed I served him. Once I realized he was there for me and he loved me, I let him. If I'm really honest, even though I went to church and believed in him, I don't think I ever gave much back to him until I matured.

The best part of this is he never failed me even though the relationship was immaturely selfish and one-sided on my part for many years. I believe he was just glad that I turned to him and saw him as the loving someone who could help me.

My point is I believed in God because that's what I was taught, but I didn't really, truly feel God until I really needed him and let him in. I could have had a million people tell me he existed and I should believe in him, but it wasn't until I felt sad, lonely, and helpless that I felt him—really felt him and let him in. What's so striking is I'm not even sure I really went to him during that time; I thought I was talking within myself and realized somewhere along the way I was talking with him. I now know he was there all along, patiently loving, patiently waiting on me to reach for his hand ... or most likely ready to grab my hand when he knew I needed him.

I started seeing hope in every situation I "spoke" with him about. Even though there were long periods of time between needing him and talking to him, I believe he was always there watching over me and waiting for me to engage with him.

I have had so many examples of him being there for me that I have grown tremendously in my faith over the years, so I talk to him on and off all day. I have been alive long enough to have had some very serious things happen to me and to people I love. He has been there for me through many big things and more small things than I could ever have enough time to list.

I went to him deeply when my brother was in a horrific car accident and in such critical condition he had to be airlifted to the closest hospital. The doctors told my family and me he had little to no chance of survival, and if he did survive, he would have no quality of life. They told us to be careful what we prayed for because if he lived, he would probably have to be taken care of for the rest of his life. My sweet mom, who has shown me so much about faith, gave me one of the most beautiful examples of faith I've ever seen. She believed God would answer her prayers about my brother, barely leaving the hospital chapel during his critical care. She prayed, and she taught all our family that God is the super tool when you need a miracle. She taught us that God is the one who decides how the story is going to end. We all desperately prayed for a happy ending even though there seemed to be no hope—and God gave us a miracle. Today, my brother is alive, doing very well, and living a beautiful, normal life!

When my dad had lung cancer and was dying, we all asked God for more time. The doctors had said he had only months to live, but with our broken hearts, we prayed hard and asked God for more time. God answered those prayers with years instead of months, which was much more than science and doctors believed he had. That's how I know a superpower was involved. The day my father passed away, he waited for me to fly across the country, and my prayers to hold his hand as he took his very last breath were answered. What should have felt like one of the scariest and worst days of my life instead felt like a beautiful, spiritual present. It's something you could never understand unless you're someone who has also been in the same situation and has a strong faith in God. I truly felt God's beautiful and magnificent presence as my dad slipped away. Instead of feeling horror and despair like I thought I would, I felt comforted and at peace. Even with faith, I never realized death could be beautiful if God was involved.

I have needed comfort, peace, and miracles from God many times, and he has delivered over and over and over again, and that's why I know he exists and why he is my superpower.

Embarrassingly, I have asked God for some pretty silly things too, which just gave my life a better day, and he blessed me with them. I believe he answered even my silly prayers to enhance my belief in him, and it has worked! His blessings make me feel his presence. His blessings time and time again have me living with such a grateful heart. My relationship with him has authentically developed over my lifetime. It has made me feel hopeful in the gravest circumstances. It has kept me from feeling all alone with my troubles. My faith has grown so much over the years that I can't imagine getting through life without having the strength of God for me and within me.

Our minds are very powerful; we can torture ourselves with thoughts and feelings that follow the many life struggles we have to face. Also, because we're humans, we're flawed, we make big mistakes, we hurt people, and other people hurt us. Stress from these situations can steal your joy that you are meant to have, and the stress can cause you emotional and physical harm. You deserve to be comforted and strengthened for your journey. You deserve a life compass. God is a great compass. You deserve to have superpowers when you need them. God is a superpower.

I can't promise you that you won't have struggles, but I can promise you if you have God in your life, they will be bearable. Where there is God, there is hope and light and strength. You have peace, comfort, and joy waiting for you from God that you get to feel when you are ready. God is not judgmental. He will be there for you whether you practice a certain religion or not. He will be there even if you don't believe in him. He will be there whether you belong to a church, go to church, study the Bible, or don't study the Bible. He will be there for you and love you no matter what. He will be there for you even when you make mistakes—big mistakes! You don't have to be perfect for him to love you and be there for you. He is also very patient. He even understands that we will be selfish and sometimes only go to him at certain times in our lives. He is the best kind of friend we could ever hope for. He does know us personally. He doesn't judge us and he loves us unconditionally whether we acknowledge it or not. As humans, we think that's a crazy concept to allow ourselves to feel and believe.

It isn't until we open ourselves up to him—go to him and tell him our requests, our stresses, our fears, our struggles, and our anxieties— that we really *feel* him respond. Once you see prayers answered, it will bring peace into your mind, and in your heart, you will realize, "Wow, he really does know me. He really does listen to me. I really do have a relationship here. He is here for me." We all get there *if and when we want*, and it's not for anyone to judge. If God doesn't judge, no one else should think we have that right.

I was very hesitant to put this chapter about faith in my book because we should all respect people's beliefs. If you don't believe, I respect your right. We all believe or don't believe based on our life experiences. I also didn't want to say the wrong thing that would make someone not want to pursue a relationship with God.

However, I wrote this book because I wanted to help you and young women have more peace and joy in your journey of growing up and in your life. I'm just trying to share all the tools that have helped me. He has given me so much comfort and direction in my life. I just couldn't write a book to help young women that didn't include him, because he has been my number-one helper! When I think about every hard thing I have ever gotten through, I cannot think of how I got through it without remembering God answered prayers for me—and if he didn't think what I was asking for was right for me, he gave me peace and comfort regarding the situation until he gifted something better for me.

You are going through things right now and will continue to go through hard times. There will be times you feel inadequate, unloved, lonely, stressed, disappointed, worried, afraid—and broken. There will be times you aren't sure who you can really trust not to repeat your words or judge your feelings or actions. There will be times you won't want to disappoint or worry someone else with what you're thinking and feeling. Because God has been "that person" for me and brought me so much strength and comfort through my life, I wanted to share that with you for your consideration.

Of course, what you want to believe or how you want to receive my message is totally up to you—but if I really want to help you, I have to share the most valuable life tool I know. My relationship with God is my most valuable life tool. He doesn't want our lives to be filled with worry. He has a purpose for us and doesn't want it blocked because of hopelessness and fear. He has gotten me through life with abundant joy even in the worst of times.

Even more unbelievably beautiful, he has brought so many beautiful blessings into my life without me even asking. The more I have become aware of him and his blessings for me, the more he has brought me. That is another beautiful thing about his relationship with us. He is so giving. He's not the kind of friend who only does something nice for you in return for what you've done for him. Trust me, I have done much less for him than he has done for me. Because he has been so good, he makes me want to grow closer to him. He always kept giving long before I got there.

As girls, we worry about so much. We worry about the way we look even though we know we shouldn't. We worry about achieving everything we think we're supposed to achieve. We worry about our friendships and our family relationships. We worry about being strong. We worry about being enough. We worry about being liked or not liked. We worry about being loved or not loved. I don't want you to worry so much. God doesn't want you to worry. I know you will because that's how girls are wired, and all the messages coming at you from all over the world and our country and our society leave you very anxious. All of it can make you feel very weary, tired, stressed, and depressed.

If you're open to it, try asking God to carry your burden and to take these worries off your shoulders. You will be amazed at how much less of that load you feel. You will be amazed at the guidance he gives your path. You will be amazed at how much more joyful you feel when you are talking to him. You will never have another relationship so trusting and loving and nonjudgmental. You deserve to feel hope and joy among all the struggles you're dealing with now and will come across on your journey of life.

A relationship with God feels beautiful. It fills your heart with enormous joy, your mind with unimaginable peace, your body with amazing strength, and your life with radiant, beautiful light!

Because of your own personal beliefs, maybe you just don't connect with what I'm saying—that's okay. We all can only follow what feels right and rings true for us. I'm not pushing God on you—I don't think he would even want me to do that. I'm just trying to help you with tools that I know and that have helped me grow in strength. You may have a different belief system. Maybe you don't have one at all. The point of this chapter is to encourage you to always have some kind of faith in a higher power in life, because then you won't feel loneliness or despair with your burdens. Where you find faith, you will have hope.

Faith in God is one kind of faith in a higher power than yourself. There are many other kinds of faith that people believe in, and I respect that. There are even kinds of faith and inspiration that I know to be very powerful for me and for others. Faith in the universe, and faith that we are all connected to one another, is something else to add to your thoughts and tools of faith. When your burdens feel heavier and bigger than you can handle, I want you to have faith you are never really alone and you're connected to higher powers and energy that can help calm you, renew you, and give you strength.

Open your heart and mind to the energy of the sun, the sky, the moon, the trees, the water, and the stars! We are connected to them, and they are powerful and magical and have renewing energy for you and for all of us. Have faith that you can draw from the powerful forces of our universe. Take a problem for a walk in the sunshine. When you feel down, wrap yourself in a blanket, and stare up at the twinkling stars. Ask the magical powers of the universe for what you need, and see if you don't feel a little better and stronger each time.

I truly believe we are all connected as people in our universe. Have faith that even though we may not all know each other, there are so many of us surrounding you with our love. We hurt when you hurt. There are also good people waiting to help you in your life. I hope you will try hard to recognize who they are. There are many good people in the world you don't even know who send out positive, loving energy toward you that you can draw from. Have faith it's there, and open yourself up to receive it. Let it calm you and build you as you believe in and feel our connection. Have faith that some of us will even be brought directly into your life to help you with whatever you're going through. Maybe my book is something you needed and it's helpful to you—and that's why it landed in your hands. Have faith that the universe connects everything and all of us and that you are never alone. You don't have to work so hard all by yourself; have faith.

Grow yourself less alone. Grow yourself less stressed and worried. Grow yourself strong and beautiful with faith.

Grow yourself beautiful.

> Have no anxiety about anything, but in everything by prayer and supplication with thanksgiving let your requests be made known to God.
> —Philippians 4:6 (RSV)

> She is clothed with strength and dignity: she can laugh at the days to come.
> —Proverb 31:25 (NIV)

> A human being is part of the whole called by us universe, a part limited in time and space. He experiences himself, his thoughts and feeling as something separated from the rest, a kind of optical delusion of his consciousness. This delusion is a kind of prison for us, restricting us to our personal desires and to affection for a few persons nearest to us. Our task must be to free ourselves from this prison by widening our circle of compassion to embrace all living creatures and the whole of nature in its beauty.
> —Albert Einstein (Goodreads.com, Albert Einstein quotes)

> In all things of nature there is something of the marvelous.
> —Aristotle (Goodreads.com, Aristotle quotes)

Eight

The most beautiful and powerful
women in the world take good care of
themselves—mind, body, and soul.

Grow Yourself B-E-A-U-T-I-F-**U**-L
U Is for Understanding Self-Care
Taking Good Care of Yourself Is Beautiful

You are not a machine or a plastic doll. You are a beautiful, living, breathing human being that needs nourishment for your mind, body, and soul. So many high expectations of you from outside sources and many from yourself! You need to take care of yourself, and no one can take care of you quite like you! Self-care is a necessity to growing yourself strong and beautiful. Self-care is a necessity to *feeling* strong and beautiful! Self-care plays a big part in growing your self-love and self-respect. Empower yourself to learn how to nurture yourself and show yourself that you are worthy of your time, love, and care.

This book is about growing yourself and empowering yourself—and self-care is paramount in that process! If you constantly chase goals and achievements with a lot of busyness—spending thoughts, time, and energy toward meeting expectations and not doing self-care—you will feel depleted, negative, off-balance, sad, exhausted, stressed, and anxious, and many other negative emotions. How often have you wondered, "Why don't I feel good or feel I'm enough if am I trying so hard and doing my best?" You probably feel this way because you've neglected your self-care. Self-care is how you will feed and nourish yourself for your journey.

Your mind, body, and soul make up your whole you. You have to feed, nourish, and grow all three of those parts of you. If you are feeding just one of those, you'll feel out of balance. You can't water just one petal on a flower, not getting anything to the roots or body of the plant, and expect it to keep flowering! You can't just concentrate on the outside, or else you will feel weak and off-balance. You have to concentrate on your inside too—that builds your strong stem and roots! Empower yourself to take care of your whole being so you can be strong and beautiful and, most importantly, *feel* strong and beautiful inside and out.

FEED AND NOURISH YOUR MIND, BODY, AND SOUL WITH FOOD

There is nothing better for your mind, body, and soul than healthy, nutritious eating. The foods you eat play an important role in how you feel, function, and look. So many of you precious girls are being taught through twisted messages from society to value being very thin. Everywhere you turn, someone is telling you how to lose weight or trying to sell you beauty products and clothes with the thinnest of thin models. Some of your friends have become so obsessed with being very thin that you often feel left out if that isn't a value for you. Some girls even discriminate against you if you aren't super thin in your natural body frame. Too many girls choose being very thin over being healthy. It breaks my heart that some people even judge young girls struggling with that, thinking it's about vanity, but they are just victims of what society has convinced them they need to be.

It's my hope that girls will learn the importance of valuing their health before all. I have important and valuable information to share with your very smart self, so please listen carefully. You can eat and be thin! You can eat and have a healthy body weight—and you don't need to be thin to be beautiful! That's such an important lesson that I want to tell you that again: you do not need to be thin to be beautiful! Beauty comes in all body types, shapes, and sizes! If any people in your life make you feel bad about your body type, those people should not be in your circle until they have their values straight.

People who judge people by body type are shallow and superficial and don't understand true beauty or true health. You should not take them seriously. You of all people need to learn to be kind to yourself about your body type. That is a very important part of self-care. Your body is supposed to be unique and special. It is not an accident that you have the body you have. Empower yourself to go on the journey to learn how to love the body type you were genetically given—and then proudly own it! Body confidence is stunningly beautiful, and you can't buy any makeup, clothes, or accessories that are more beautiful than confidence! We aren't all supposed to look the same. What a boring bunch of cookie-cutter robots we would be if we did. We are created to be originals. True beauty comes from embracing yourself and growing yourself with substance and meaning.

A beautiful body is a healthy body that is fed a proper balance and variety of fruits, vegetables, lean proteins, eggs, healthy fats, whole grains, nuts, and legumes. Caring for yourself with these beautiful foods and water will grow you strong and beautiful with an energized brain, healthy and functioning internal organs, and a strong immune system. It will allow you to have the physical stamina to help your body perform at its maximum level so you can pursue your dreams.

Did you know that good food boosts your mood? It really does! It also plays a significant role in beautiful skin, nails, and hair. No amount of makeup or hair products can make your mood, hair, nails, and skin as bright and beautiful as the right food can. I want you to think more about the grocery store than the beauty counter because it will bring you what you're looking for.

No honor roll or degree represents your intelligence more than caring for yourself by feeding your brain and body properly. There is no goal more important than your self-care. Self-care will help you develop your confidence and self-love. Somewhere along the way, confusing messages about what to buy for body and beauty enhancement forgot to include the most important beauty product of all, and that is nutritious food. Nutritious food is the best brain booster, strength maker, and beauty enhancer you can buy. Self-care through nutritious food is one of the best and smartest ways to grow yourself strong and beautiful!

Before we leave the subject of food, I want to add what I call soul food to self-care. We all have certain foods in our lives that make us feel warm and safe; they're like a food hug. They may or may not be the most nutritious, but they do feed your soul. Don't deprive yourself. I personally believe it's important to add a healthy dose of your soul food here and there. Life is meant to be joyful, and food is life! Whether it's homemade chicken noodle soup or warm, homemade chocolate chip cookies that make your house smell like love, I encourage you to treat and care for yourself with your soul food. Soul food reminds us that food is nourishing to our souls and spirits as much as to our bodies. Soul food reminds us to love and nurture our whole self. It's also fun because it reminds us of the people we love who lovingly introduced those soul foods into our lives.

Knowing how to make nutritious meals and snacks for yourself is an important part of self-care. If you don't already know how, challenge yourself to begin by learning how to at least make your favorite meal and your soul food. If you know how to make your favorite meal and your soul food, you'll always have those when your mind, body, and soul crave them.

Empower yourself to learn to make nutritious and soulful foods for yourself. Keep growing those self-care cooking skills!

JUST SAY, "NO, I HAVE STUFF TOMORROW," FOR YOUR SELF-CARE

What you keep out of your body and your life is just as important as what you put in. There are so many reasons to not smoke, do drugs, or begin drinking at an early age—but the most important is it's up to you to take good care of yourself and your life. Addiction to harmful substances is real! You are not bulletproof, and you won't be "the one" it doesn't grab! If you don't have your health, you have absolutely nothing! If you have your health, you can make all your dreams come true. This isn't about the law or authority telling you not to do something. This is about you empowering yourself to take care of your body, your present self, and your future self. It's about showing yourself love and respect. You have goals, you have dreams, you have plans, and you have a beautiful life ahead. Don't put harmful substances in your body that will lead you away from them. It's you, beautiful you, who has to tell yourself that you care too much about yourself to harm you, your life, and your dreams. Just say, "No, I have stuff tomorrow." ♥

POSITIVE SELF-TALK IS IMPORTANT SELF-CARE

What we think and say to ourselves directly affects the way we feel. Make sure you send yourself healthy messages through kind thoughts and positive conversations with yourself. It's more than okay to compliment yourself on what you got right today. It's necessary to say sincere, kind, and loving things to yourself as you would to a dear friend. If you just talk down to yourself all day, your mood, self-esteem, and life will begin to reflect that.

Don't worry; humility still exists when you think lovingly of yourself. It really is okay to tell yourself you're a good person and you know that you're trying hard at life. It's important to recognize all your beautiful gifts and smile at them. It's important to be your own cheerleader and remind yourself of your strengths. It's important to compliment yourself on how far you've come in your difficult areas. The nicer and more lovingly you talk to yourself, the more confident, happier, stronger, and more beautiful you will *feel* on the inside. It will feel less important to you to chase those words and affirmations from someone else.

EXERCISE SELF-CARE BY WHO YOU SPEND YOUR TIME WITH

Another important part to self-care is monitoring the messages you allow into your body from outside sources. You won't feel good if you allow a steady flow of negative messaging to come into you. You have to be the gatekeeper of who and what you let into your mind because it can really affect your moods, body, and general health. Too much time exposed to negative people and their negative energy is harmful to you. You really have to become aware of how people make you feel. Exercise self-care by monitoring other people's energy influence in your life. Spending too much time with negative, cynical, or judgmental people is not a way to nurture and care for yourself. You have to limit your exposure to them. If you have a constant negative or toxic personality in your life, you have to let that friendship go. It doesn't have to result in some big, dramatic ending. Exercise self-care and become strong enough to let it go, but let it go in peace so you don't have drama. Some people are just not healthy in general or not healthy for us specifically, and it's important to recognize that and then let go of them. This is a very hard one—but very important for your self-care! It's very empowering and a very healthy way to live.

MONITORING MESSAGES COMING IN IS IMPORTANT TO SELF-CARE

In addition to negative people, world problems and superficial messages can take a toll on you, leaving you feeling worried and weary. Listen to enough news so you are connected to and informed of what's happening in the world, but then stop allowing a lot of it in. The world can feel like a pretty crazy place; it's healthy and necessary to block some of that out. When you do allow it in, exercise self-care by understanding not everything you're seeing and hearing is true.

As I've referenced all through this book, the world sends messages to you from so many different places. Remember that so much of what those messages say is superficial. When you see TV ads or magazine ads, remember they are just trying to sell products. Those ads are about making money, not genuinely about making you look good. Please don't let what you see in those ads greatly affect your moods or self-esteem. So much of it isn't real. You are too smart and have too much potential to stay focused on all of that! What they are selling and the way they are trying to sell it are very superficial. They will not add any kind of true beauty, joy, or meaning to your life. Becoming more aware of the messages coming at you and who is sending them to you is so very important in your self-care. Because so much of advertising is harmful, care about yourself enough to limit its access to you.

EXHIBIT MORE SELF-CARE IN YOUR SOCIAL MEDIA

While social media is meant to be fun and help you feel more socially connected, if you don't pay attention to self-care with it, it can have some very negative effects on you. I touched on some of that in the authenticity chapter, but here are some other important areas within social media where I hope you'll exercise important self-care.

Let's start here with the amount of time you spend on social media. Becoming more aware of and more disciplined about the amount of time you allow yourself on social media is vital to your self-care. Try to more consciously choose *when* and *how often* you will go on; then give yourself a time limit. An all-day, steady stream of going on and off doesn't just affect the productivity of your life; it's too much and too often for you to take on and process everything you see and feel from it. Social media and self-care have to go hand in hand for you to protect yourself. Empower yourself to be disciplined about the amount of time you allow social media into your heart and head. Otherwise, you let others have *way* too much time to influence your thoughts, feelings, energy, and moods. That's not healthy or fair to you.

There will always be too many people using social media in a negative way. You can't be willing to give them too much access to you. If you have contacts who constantly spread negativity, or just elicit feelings that don't feel good to you, consider hiding them or removing them from your friend list. You have to be your own life bouncer. We all struggle with doing that, but know you aren't doing it against just anyone; and understand you are doing it for you! You shouldn't feel like you have to follow anyone who or anything that doesn't make you feel good. That's very important to your self-care.

Another important way to exercise self-care is by remembering you are watching everyone's highlight reel on social media. Most people show their favorite or best experience of the day, week, month, or year. Take self-care and guard yourself from feelings of envy or inadequacy by remembering that it's a highlight reel. As you look at other people's social media, especially other young women's, remember that comparison is not healthy or fair to you. If it's a photo of them, they've most likely posted a perfectly angled, filtered photo after taking and throwing away fifteen other pictures. We are all girls, so we know how that works.

Regardless of what you see, everyone has bad moments, bad days, bad weeks, and bad years! All people have experiences and features they don't want to put on a highlight reel. Empower yourself to not scroll and compare. Be kind to yourself, and empower yourself to keep the wise perspective of not taking it all in at face value.

Something else I believe important to self-care is to not just be a *spectator* of other people's lives. Be a *participant* if you're choosing to spend your time on social media. I know it can feel scary putting yourself out there, but I believe you're sending yourself an unhealthy message if you mostly just watch what other people do. Come off the sidelines and out of the dark shadows, and share some of yourself doing what you do. You've been building yourself! You've been growing yourself beautiful! You're an interesting, beautiful person, and you have meaningful things to share—so you should!

And when you choose to post, empower yourself to not chase likes. It should be about you liking you and you liking what you share. Share something about yourself that shows who you are and the substance of your life so you can connect meaningfully with people. I think you'll gain more and more confidence as you share these meaningful, authentic pieces.

Too many young girls are buying into some of the self-destructive social media culture I've already talked about. We can't have you truly believing your value and worth are determined by the amount of likes you receive. You will always feel something is missing if you post hourly and daily pictures to try to prove to yourself or other people that you are pretty, popular, or sexy, no matter how many likes you get. You are too smart to measure your beauty and worth by social media likes. For your self-care, understand that many of those likes do not come from real friends or real relationships. That makes them empty likes. Even more important, many girls are willing to befriend complete strangers into all their friends' personal lives just to increase their chances for more likes. Not only do these strangers add no substance to someone's personal life, but this act can be very dangerous—and all for more likes? Empower yourself to move any strangers off your friend list. If you don't personally know them or have experience with them, they are strangers! Otherwise, you are putting you and your friends at risk, because you put enough information out there where strangers can find any of you if they want.

Really think about these things, and empower yourself to show more care for yourself in your social media. If you let likes build you up, it will hurt you and tear you down too much when you don't get them. You will always be at the mercy of someone's good nature, moods, or jealousies. Self-care means not relying on the like button to build you up and not allowing it to tear you down. Your like is what you should go for. Your like is the most meaningful and important.

Also, empower yourself to not worry about how many likes someone else gets either. Remember that these numbers just signify a total number of people and are not indicative of real, personal, loving, meaningful relationships. If you really want to build yourself up, take a look at the quality of your likes. Take note of your real relationships and how many of those people who liked your post are actually relevant to your well-being and to your life. That's where the magic is for you! That's what will feel meaningful.

Another important way to care for yourself is to never engage in cyberbullying in any way. Never cyberbully anyone else, and if you find yourself to be someone's target, don't be tempted to participate or retaliate. For whatever their reasons, sadly we all have people in our lives who use social media to be overly aggressive and passive aggressive too. If you want to give the power to you and take away theirs, don't publicly engage with them. I can't stress enough how important this is for your self-care. Participating will bring you into their negative world. Ignore, hide, or unfriend the negative and harmful people! And if that something harmful is directed at you personally, quietly report them to people who can stop them.

Thank goodness there are a lot of positive people doing a lot of positive things on social media. I hope you empower yourself to share positivity and be the light and substance the world needs. I hope you'll feel confident enough to be kind and supportive to others. If people have shared something that is important to them, show them you care about them. Leave them a comment. Build them up. Show them support. Showing loving care to others on social media shows loving care to you! Using social media in only positive ways that will strengthen your connections is important to your self-care.

Most importantly, trust yourself. If social media as a whole consistently doesn't make you feel good, maybe it's not for you. Social media is not for everyone. Don't let anyone make you feel like social media is a must. Social media is not a must. You will always be relevant in real life. In fact, not using it can give you more time for real life. Everyone has different things that make him or her feel good, and it's okay if social media is just not for you. There are many ways to connect with people that are more real and more satisfying anyway! If social media makes you feel bad, empower yourself to connect with people in other ways that bring you connection and joy.

EXERCISE SELF-CARE BY STAYING AWAY FROM DRAMA

Living in peace and harmony will make you feel strong and beautiful. Living in the girl world can be fun and beautiful, but as we noted earlier, it can also be a very dramatic, painful place for us. You can have new drama every day if you're willing to let it in. We've acknowledged girls can be very competitive and jealous as they're finding their way, their place, and their maturity. If you approach your days wanting peace and harmony for yourself, you will let more unimportant things roll off you than you ever have. There are some people who seem to always cause trouble or drama, but that doesn't mean you have to sign up for it. Try to understand that their drama is theirs—and you can separate yourself from it to keep your world beautiful.

Living in peace is essential to self-care. Try your best to not let people drag you into their messes, pettiness, or bad moods. If and when you find yourself the target of someone else's insecurities, quickly move from that person, and seek people who make you feel good and safe. Let people know by the way you handle yourself that you are a peaceful and kind person. If they don't like you, move on to find people who do. And if you find yourself involved with people who aggressively show you they don't like you, kindly ask them to stop giving you their time and attention. Set your boundaries for people. Let people know that peace, kindness, and happiness are important to you, and take care of yourself accordingly. It's almost impossible for people to keep drama alive if you're not a willing participant. Empower your world to be drama-free. You deserve a peaceful, drama-free life so you can feel powerful and beautiful!

FORGIVENESS IS IMPORTANT IN SELF-CARE

We all have people who have hurt us, whether they directly intended it or not. Sometimes we find ourselves in situations with other people who hurt us so badly we think we can never get past it. Sometimes, we are even the person who has hurt someone else, and that makes us feel terrible. Human beings are flawed, and we all make a lot of mistakes. The best thing we can do is live with humility, keep learning from our mistakes, and be determined to grow into better people. It's so important to reflect on and learn from your mistakes but then forgive yourself for making them. Mistakes are a part of life.

It's also very important to forgive others. Think of those people you know who are always angry and hold on to bitterness. It seems they remember every wrong they've ever encountered and want to make the rest of us pay for it. They forget that they, too, have made mistakes and hurt others. You don't want that to be you. It shows true strength and true beauty when you forgive yourself or someone else.

Forgiveness does not mean you have to allow the same hurt to continue, or continue to let the same people hurt you. It does mean that you will not continue to live in that same place of hurt. You will not let it eat you up or make you feel sad and stuck. Forgive, keep the lessons, and grow toward a better place. People who forgive make room for beautiful feelings in their lives. Forgiveness takes strength but builds more strength; forgiveness is beautiful.

GROW IN YOUR HUMILITY

Humility is a beautiful virtue. It's also a virtue that has a way of taking a lot of pressure off you. Having a strong sense of self and caring for yourself are very different from being self-important. Humility doesn't mean putting yourself down or making yourself unimportant; it means showing people you know that you have a lot to learn—we all do! Humility shows other people that you value them and their circumstances and that you don't just care about your well-being. If the whole world were self-important, none of us would ever feel very good.

Show appreciation for your life and people in your life. Recognizing other people have needs and appreciating other people is important in their care and your self-care. Living with humility will help you form meaningful bonds with people. Living with humility will always connect you with humanity at a deep, meaningful level. When you're wrong, recognize it and apologize for it. When you live with humility and don't go around acting all self-important, it allows you forgiveness when you make honest and human mistakes. People are much more willing to be in your corner and lift you up when you live with genuine humility. You can be confident and show humility at the same time. Stay open to learning, and know you still have so many ways to keep learning and growing—that's humility. Humility is beautiful.

QUIET TIME IS IMPORTANT IN YOUR SELF-CARE

Feed your mind, body, and soul with quiet, just-me time as part of the unplugged time we already talked about. How will you ever know how you really feel if you're always listening to outside sources? Get in touch with yourself and create your own energy by feeding your mind, body, and soul with quiet me time. You will have busy days when having quiet time for yourself may seem impossible. Those are probably some of the most important days to give yourself some quiet.

At the very least, try to take five minutes for yourself in a quiet spot—close your eyes and try to relax. Quiet your mind, and try to keep it free from racing thoughts. During that time, breathe deep, full, cleansing breaths. Giving yourself time for quiet, mindful meditation where you just allow yourself to be in that moment is so healthy. Doing nothing but breathing and existing can calm you down. Maybe even put one positive word in your head, like *beautiful* or *peace*. It can put you in touch with yourself and help you feel more centered and peaceful. Try to work this into every day. Whether it's two minutes, an hour, or more, quiet time is so important to your mental health. Taking care of your mental health is key to self-care, and this is just one more important and easy way to do that. Once you find out how well this really works, look up some more tips for meditation, and learn methods that you can really enjoy. Quiet time and meditation are powerful self-care tools. I have included resources at the back of my book for you to explore meditation.

EXERCISE IS IMPORTANT TO SELF-CARE

Exercising is also a very nurturing thing to do for you. Exercise not only builds a healthy body, it also significantly boosts your brainpower and mood. It can build your health in so many ways— mentally and physically! It can keep you from getting sick, reduce stress, and help you sleep better. Use exercise to show yourself how much you love and value your body, strength, and health. It's important to approach exercise as a gift for yourself, rather than a punishment or a debt you have to suffer through for something you ate. There are all kinds of exercise; it doesn't have to feel like intense work, so just find something that makes you move that you enjoy. Make a list of different types of physical activity that make you feel good, and mix it up. You could walk or hike through nature, run, do yoga, bike or spin, dance, swim, lift weights, do Tai Chi, box, or do any sport. Exercise will make you feel important to yourself! Exercise is a form of self-respect and very important to self-care. Exercise makes you feel strong and beautiful.

TIME SPENT GROOMING YOURSELF IS SELF-CARE

Treat yourself like someone special. Giving self-care to your hair, skin, and nails may sound silly, but it will help you build your self-esteem and grow your self-love. This is your "birthday suit," your original fashion statement that will always be with you.

When you're at home, give yourself a clean face, and moisturize it. You'll be surprised how beautiful it makes you feel. I know you have many messages coming at you about makeup, and if it makes you feel good to wear it, then you should. However, when you're home, treat your face with importance; clean skin will make you feel beautiful and fresh.

When you feel stressed or just want to feel nurtured, treat yourself to a bubble bath with moisturizing and scented oils. Remember how much fun bubble baths were when you were little and how joyful they made you feel? This special time for yourself, created by yourself, will calm you down and make you feel important. It's time with yourself to unplug and rejuvenate.

Sometimes we have great hair days, and sometimes your hair will have a mind of its own. That's just the way hair naturally goes! However, if you care for your hair daily, it's more likely to make than to break most of your days. Whatever the style that suits its mood, your mood, or the occasion for the day, show yourself that you care about your hair before you expect it to perform. You can't always control it in every way, but the more you care for it through eating healthy foods, performing daily hygiene, and combing, brushing, and styling it, the more you show yourself you care for you! How you treat your hair can truly affect the way you feel inside. Everyone's hair and activities are different, so there are no right or wrong rules—just what's best for your hair that day. Take the time to try to figure that out. Whether it's a straightened, curly, ponytail, or messy bun kind of day, show yourself you are special by being well groomed. It will bring you growing confidence and self-love and make you feel a sense of control over your day.

Don't forget to care for your hands, feet, and nails too even when it's not a special occasion. Remember you are working on the way you *feel*, not just the way you look. This may also sound like a silly, unimportant thing, but learning to take regular, special care of them will make you feel nurtured and beautiful. Test what I'm saying by caring for your hands, feet, and nails; make sure you're clean here too and your nails are nicely trimmed. If you want to really feel the love, take it a few steps further, and moisturize them. You cannot apply lotion to your hands and feet without feeling special and nurtured; it's such a simple hug for yourself. Also, if it makes you feel good to have your nails painted, develop your skill in painting them yourself. Listen to your favorite music while doing it, and it may become one of your favorite self-love rituals. I know you may not feel like you are the greatest at painting them, but the more you do it, the better you will get; plus it's about the kind and loving experience. Becoming good at painting your own nails is a funny skill that brings about a surprising confidence. When you look at your hands and feet and see the care you've given them, you send yourself the message that you are important and cared for. Self-care shown to your hands, feet, and nails is an underestimated, beautiful way to nurture yourself and grow in your self-esteem. Having said that, remember that something as small as chipped nail polish can make you feel messy or unorganized, so follow through on treating yourself in a special way, and take it off before it gets too chipped.

Learning how to pamper and care for your birthday suit in all these many ways will help you feel genuinely polished and nurtured. Give it a try!

"CREATE YOUR SPACE" FOR SELF-CARE

You couldn't have convinced me of this when I was younger, but when your personal spaces are organized and tidy, you will feel that way inside too! Set time aside to have your room, workspaces, and bathroom reflect how organized and centered you want to feel. If everything is all out of order and jumbled, your mind will feel like that too! If you change your mindset from "having to clean" to "creating my space," it will feel much more rewarding and nurturing than a chore.

Get in the habit of making your bed. It will immediately make your room as a whole feel more organized and give you a sense of control for your day. Your bed will also feel fresh when you climb back in. Eliminate the piles of clutter. Organize your stuff. Clean the yuck. Keep your important items looking important. Bring your favorite colors into your space. Have art and music items and a place where you can be creative when you want to be. Surround yourself with cozy items that feel soft and comforting for your quiet times. All these loving touches in creating your space will really allow a settled, cozy feeling. You deserve a grounding sanctuary!

A STRONG AND SMART WORK ETHIC IS IMPORTANT IN SELF-CARE

So many people will try to tell you what it means to be successful, but your loving yourself, loving your life, and loving what you do with your life will bring your greatest feeling of success. Take time to dream and picture what you want for yourself and for your life. Empower yourself to make your dreams come true. Empower yourself to work to make that happen for you. Anything worthwhile takes time and effort—and being a woman who knows what she wants and is willing to work hard for it is powerful and beautiful! Staying on top of what you're working toward will always make you feel strong and capable, so don't procrastinate.

Procrastinating and not working efficiently will make you feel overwhelmed and like you're drowning in responsibilities. Empower yourself to not let your responsibilities pile up. Stay on top of them so you can stay strong in your journey toward everything you want your life to be. Part of self-care is learning to carve your goals into small, achievable pieces so that you can enjoy your journey to fulfilling your dreams. Being disciplined with your time will allow you to have time to work hard but also allow you the time for having balance and nurturing yourself.

Try to remember working toward goals isn't working to exhaustion; it's working smart, so be strategic with your time and schedule and self-care. Long, tiring hours will be necessary at times. That is part of having a strong work ethic. But when you have time to rest, rest. Make sure you understand that *rest* is very productive too. For good self-care in your journey, it's good to frequently evaluate the way you work. You really can alleviate stress just by knowing that you are working hard and smart. Working hard and smart is the best you can do—so try to relax more, and just stay focused on what you want to accomplish ... in pieces.

As I have said in earlier parts of this book, you don't have to be many things already. You are empowering yourself to grow in strength and meaningful beauty along the way. You need to have strength for this journey, and your self-care will keep you feeling nourished and strong. As you do all you need to do to care for yourself, you will also grow in your self-respect and self-love. You will feel strong because you will begin to realize that you hold the key to how you *feel*. You will empower yourself to allow yourself time to become anything you want to be, not what other people want you to be or think you should be. You will also understand that you don't have to be so many things already.

You're acknowledging how individual and special you already are, and self-care proves it! You get to be on a journey of growth your whole life. You especially deserve the important time for this journey from a girl to a woman. Taking care of yourself is the most beautiful, strengthening thing you can do. You deserve this time for self-care to develop your strong foundation. It's your foundation that will give you your strength and assure you of your true beauty. If you empower yourself to grow yourself beautiful through self-care, you will ooze strength and beauty, and you will be able to share your beauty with others. Self-care will not only build you up but also give you strength and beauty to build up others too.

Self-care is powerful. Self-care is beautiful.

Grow yourself beautiful.

Nine

The most beautiful and powerful women in the world share abundant love with themselves and with the world.

Grow Yourself B-E-A-U-T-I-F-U-**L**
L Is for Love
Loving Yourself and Sharing Your Love Is Beautiful

WHERE THERE IS LOVE, THERE IS BEAUTY, STRENGTH, AND JOY

Love. I saved the best for last! If you truly want to grow yourself in ways that make you *feel* strong and beautiful, loving yourself and loving others provide the most important nutrients and sunshine for your life. Sharing love will always bring you beauty, meaning, and joy. Let's fill you and your life with lots and lots of love—self-love, family love, friend love, girl-power love, community love, big-world love! When you fill your world with love, everything is more beautiful. There isn't anyone in the world who doesn't want or need love. Love is the universal language that we all understand, and it connects us to each other. It's pretty cool because it's something that's capable of both calming and exciting a person or situation. Love is like food that brings nutrients to your heart and life and to all those you touch.

Every time a situation contains love, it brings beauty, light, hope, and life. When you've been your happiest self, I'm willing to bet love was involved, coming from you and to you and around you. I'm also willing to bet in your highest times of anxiety, stress, or loneliness, you felt love was missing, you were about to lose it, or it wouldn't come. You may have even had times where you felt like you had love to give but no one really wanted or appreciated yours.

When we feel loved, it makes us feel safe, fulfilled, and complete. It makes us feel like we are enough. I believe that we have a deep need to share our love with others too. To love and to be loved is at the heart of your happiness, security, and connections. If you want to help yourself feel complete, help others thrive and help us all get along by cultivating love. It all begins with cultivating love within yourself, your inner voice, your outer words, your actions, and your life with as much importance and nourishment as what you eat and how you breathe. Love is as important to sustaining you as air and food. Begin to pay attention to how you give love to yourself and others and receive it.

Begin with self-love because that's the key to your happiness and the foundation for all the other kinds. It's difficult to give and receive love if your self-love is not there first. I know you've probably heard the term *self-love* a lot, but you're probably also a little confused as to what self-love actually means. You may even wonder if you have it. You may wonder if you have enough. You may wonder how to develop it. I will give you my definition for the purpose of trying to understand what it can mean for you and how you can grow it. I believe self-love is a soft, humble acceptance of who and what you are. It's a caring desire to make loving, healthy, nurturing, and kind choices for yourself. Self-love is a lifelong, loving conversation and journey with yourself. Self-love is what allows you to *feel* truly beautiful inside and out.

Ever since you were little, I know you've been bombarded with outside messages that can leave you feeling so imperfect, unsafe, unworthy, or even embarrassed to love yourself. Much of your stress has come from wanting to be loved and not knowing if that love is coming. You worry whether you can love yourself, and you worry if other people will love you. The answer is yes. You are very worthy of love, and yes, it's there, and yes, more will come. It takes time to grow in your self-love, but it only takes a day to show yourself you care; then you're on your way. As you grow in self-love, you will see and know that you are lovable to others too!

Self-love is that kind, loving conversation with yourself—backed up by the loving choices you make for yourself throughout a day. From the first thoughts of your day to the gratitude you acknowledge before closing your eyes, it can be a really fun process! Self-love feels so nurturing, loving, and kind to yourself. *Grow Yourself Beautiful* is all about ideas for conversations and choices you can make for and with yourself that are loving, healthy, nurturing, and kind. Those ideas and choices are what show and grow your self-love. Self-love is the surest and most perfect way to *grow yourself beautiful*!

Empower yourself to take the time to learn how lovable you are. Empower yourself to show yourself how worthy of self-love you are. No one else can do that for you. Others can tell you that they want that for you, but only you can convince yourself you're worth it. Only you can empower yourself to love yourself—and only you can grow your self-love. It's a journey full of loving, beautiful choices you get to make that feel so good!

Empower yourself to start your loving conversations and loving choices beginning right now. If you've struggled with it in the past, let the past be in the past. Start focusing on allowing yourself to love and accept everything about you, including what you think are imperfections. Begin to softly accept and appreciate all the pieces of you, letting them remind you that they are qualities and characteristics that make you a unique, special, and magnificent whole. Accept that they allow you to be special, more loving, compassionate, and humble—all beautiful qualities.

Empower yourself to love your past and present struggles. They have made you beautifully strong. Empower yourself to love your past mistakes. The lessons learned have made you wiser and have given your life a stronger, more positive direction. Empower yourself to love yourself because it's that love that will draw even more love to you from you and from others. It's also that love that will inspire you to share your love and build you and your life with meaning. You're very lovable in so many special and unique ways. Show yourself—keep growing yourself!

THROW LOVE AT CHALLENGING SITUATIONS SO YOU GET TO LIVE IN A BEAUTIFUL ENVIRONMENT

Giving and receiving love at times flows so naturally in our life, but other times, it's hard and it takes strength and commitment to love. I'm sure at times you've had to reach deep to find love in some situations and areas of your life. There are just those difficult times, sometimes with difficult people, that make bringing love to a situation a really challenging thing to do.

The purpose of this particular lesson is so that you can become more aware of creating a loving world for yourself. Other people will always do things that hurt and anger you, but I want you to grow in your awareness of where it's important to your life to not add fuel to the fire. I want you to grow in your awareness of where you can make *your world* a safer, more joyful place by choosing loving responses in those tough circumstances.

Throughout a day, you may have some challenging situations in your personal, school, or work relationships—or maybe with a random stranger over a parking space. Try to think back to some specific times in your life where someone was rude to you, disappointed you, neglected you, disrespected you, excluded you, or talked bad about you and maybe even screamed at you. I know it hurt you and made you feel terrible. It probably made you want to defend yourself by being rude or hurtful back. If you did lash back, I bet it caused you additional stress, drama, hurt, and maybe loneliness too. It's very normal to want to fight right back with the same behavior that hurt us in the first place. The problem with matching dark and hate with dark and hate is that it always causes you additional pain. It always brings more stress with it. It may make you feel powerful for a quick minute, but it leaves you feeling worse on top of what originally happened. That's a hard but important lesson to learn along the way. Those situations have happened to all of us, and I want you to remember how bad those reactions made you feel, because it's hard to build yourself strong and beautiful if you regularly allow unloving, challenging situations to draw you in, bog you down, and make you feel stressed and dark. Being angry for too long in dark situations makes your world feel the same way. Try to start thinking of love as light for these situations.

As a gift to yourself, try to have more determination to bring love to the hardest of times to help turn them around. Love is a magical and more powerful tool. Sometimes it even helps to think of it as a powerful weapon that builds rather than destroys. Take the time to feel the feelings that came from the way someone mistreated you. Breathe. Relax. Calm yourself before you respond. Decide what you want to bring into your life and what you want to keep out. People mistreat us for many reasons, but usually, it's a lack of love and light in their life. Many people come from unloving lives and don't have the love and support that you do. Rather than adding to their love deficiency, try to increase the amount of love in your life (and theirs) by answering those tough situations with love. Sometimes you can even demonstrate that love by giving no response at all.

No one has the right to hurt you in any way. You should always be willing to stand up for yourself and be your fiercest protector by showing people how you want and deserve to be treated. However, I encourage you to take time to carefully and lovingly respond when it involves a situation or relationship that is important for you to turn around. Think back to a specific situation where you waited until you thought it was worth it to approach the situation with light and love. I bet that loving approach made it possible to positively diffuse or build the situation. It's the love that turned it around. Love brings light to difficult situations. Love brings you closer to how you want that situation resolved.

Empower yourself to throw love into the tough situations that are worth it for you. Empower yourself to create a healthy, beautiful, loving environment for yourself. Love gives you a sense of control over a situation because love is powerful. Everywhere you want love, empower yourself to bring love and spread love. It's not always easy, but if the situation is worth it to you, then you should lovingly respond to it. The places where your love feels wasted are not the right places for you to stay. Love yourself enough to recognize those situations.

BRING YOUR LOVE TO THE GIRL WORLD, ESPECIALLY YOUR SELF-LOVE

In the kindness chapter, we already acknowledged how important it is to bring more kindness into the girl world, especially because having a circle of loving and supportive girlfriends is a life necessity for us! The more love and kindness you can bring into your friendships, the fewer troubles and the healthier friendships you'll have. Because girls can cause each other a lot of stress through mean behavior, don't forget to bring yourself some extra love and kindness to help you grow through painful times.

Among our closest circles, we all have times when our friends treat us badly. Out of nowhere, you're suddenly excluded or you find out you're being talked badly about behind your back. Maybe you even find yourself in a "frenemy" competition you didn't know existed or want to be in. I hope you'll try to honestly analyze and check yourself to make sure you bring love and healthy behaviors into your friendships. If you don't, you'll never have the results you want. But sometimes you're going to be treated poorly, and it will have absolutely nothing to do with you or anything you've done—and everything to do with the girl who's treating you that way. When you know you've been a good friend, empower yourself to understand it's because of something the other girl lacks and there's no need to blame yourself. I want you to learn to love yourself by recognizing those situations and not letting them tear you down.

Sometimes girls and even grown women don't know how to love themselves yet, and that's why they aren't good friends to you. This may be an example of them not having the same kind of love and support surrounding them that you do. Girls like that are on their own journey of self-love too and maybe haven't gotten as secure as you. They have work to do to develop more in their self-love so that they can become more loving people for themselves and other people. They may treat you a certain way—or try to paint you a certain way to others—because they think it will make them feel better about themselves; it won't. So find your power in knowing that, and don't allow yourself to be a victim.

I know it feels terrible to get hurt by anyone, and especially by someone you consider a close friend. It's okay to be sad and feel down for a while about the situation. Feel all those feelings that come from that hurt and disappointment; that's really important to do. However, get up and empower yourself to stay strong on your journey of self-love. Try hard to recognize and understand others' ugly and poor behavior is about them, not you. You are growing yourself beautiful, so you are rising above the tough circumstance and moving toward positive relationships because of your self-love.

When you feel mistreated by others, recognizing their behavior is about them and *not* about you will be a powerful game changer for you. Try to leave their behavior alone, and let it be about them. Shift your focus to shining your light and love on you! Stay determined to not let them and their behaviors get in the way of your self-love. Don't dull your sparkle. Don't dim your light. Don't hide your confidence. Don't be afraid to keep expressing yourself authentically. Don't stop chasing all the things that are important to you. Don't allow their behavior to make you feel like you are too much or not enough. You don't need to diminish your gifts to try to get them to like you or love you. Shift your focus from them, and concentrate on all that you are that makes you feel good. Keep a loving conversation with yourself about it all. Let them go on their own journey, and be determined to stay on course with yours. Keep your love, keep your power, and keep your beauty as you're going through these things with other girls. I know that's not easy to do, but you will grow yourself beautiful and proud and strong!

I believe the reason you have to encounter some of these difficult girls and difficult experiences with them is to help you develop your resilience and your love—love *for yourself* and love *for others*. I really think it helps you figure out the kind of woman you don't want to become just as much as it directs you to the kind of woman you *do* want to become.

Developing unwavering self-love is a journey, especially because so many things make you question it along the way, especially in dealing with other girls. Self-love is critical for building yourself strong, feeling beautiful, feeling joy, and sharing love. You need self-love before you can be a great friend to other girls. As we've discussed, that's exactly why some girls are terrible to other girls. It takes self-love to be able to develop meaningful, loving, lasting relationships. You're reading this book because you want to learn ways to grow stronger and more meaningfully beautiful, so that's proof that you're committed to loving yourself. That's also proof that you want to become a loving friend to other people. As you grow yourself beautiful, you will be able to tell which women lack in self-love by the way they treat others. *Girls and women who have self-love will always treat each other better than the ones who don't.*

Empower yourself to not chase friends or girls who don't make you and your world feel filled with love. I know you want to be part of them, but if they hurt you, they're not good for you or right for you. The way you treat yourself and define yourself will let you know what feels right or wrong to you. No one else's opinion of you or behavior toward you should dictate the way you feel about yourself. Only you should have that power. Self-love is that power! Other people's feedback, opinion, and treatment of you are a reflection of how they feel about themselves.

When you're on the receiving end of someone not loving you the way you deserve, empower yourself to love that friendship for the lessons, and let it grow you in even more determination of your self-love. Try your best to even feel compassion for that person. Compassion for others is very powerful. Send loving thoughts such people's way as you move away from them so you aren't burdened by ugly, bad thoughts. When you possess the ability to do that, it will make you feel powerful and beautiful. Keep yourself moving toward mutually loving relationships. Keep trying to seek out the lovers and your supporters as you build your friend circle. I promise they're there. You won't see them if you allow yourself to stay stuck with people who aren't good for you. The lovers and supporters are the friends who you should spend time with and who will assist you in the growing and building of you—and you will do the same for them!

Grow into the kind of woman who supports and shares love with other women. Those are the beautiful women of our world! Those are the powerful women in our world! Those are the women who make a difference in the world! Bring love to the girls in the world. Friendships should not feel like torture. You don't have to be close to unloving girls just to have friends. If you are a loving person, you will always have friends. Keep yourself moving toward girls and women who support your self-love and bring love to you. Support other girls the way you want to be supported. Strong and beautiful women lift others—you are growing yourself strong and beautiful!

When you find the friends who lift you up and encourage you—who don't feel the need to diminish you or compete with you—make sure you are also a very loving friend to them in return. So many people take loving friends for granted and chase the love of the ones who don't send it back. That is something weird about human nature. Let's not chase people who don't see our value or treat us well. Supportive, true friends aren't always easy to find, so be sure not to take your loving friends for granted or ignore them for others. Keep them feeling special, and keep the love flowing to them so you don't lose them. They have made an investment in you, so give them lots of love and support. This will help protect the friendships and make them loving, healthy relationships for all of you. Having good people to hold our hands and support us through life is so important. Good friendships don't happen or last unless we approach them with love and keep it going. That love begins with us. Bring love to yourself! Bring loving behaviors into your friendships! Bring love to the girl world!

BRING YOUR SELF-LOVE WHEN MAKING DECISIONS ABOUT SEX

This is a very important topic for you. The topic of sex is also a very personal matter, much like political and religious beliefs, so I will just lightly touch on this subject. My message on this will be short, but it's incredibly, incredibly important. I want this message to help protect you from heartbreaking regrets, consequences that cannot be reversed, and self-destructive guilt. Please take special note here—your body is your personal treasure. Your body is your most important treasure! It belongs to you and no one else. When you decide you want to share it with someone else, make sure you understand that you will not only be giving your body—you will be giving your heart too.

The way we are wired as girls and women makes it very difficult to engage in sex and not have our hearts attached to it. For the sake of your heart and your self-esteem, do not share your body in order to try to get someone to like you or love you. You should only share your body when you are certain you have had a long-enough history with that person to trust you both share love and respect. You deserve and need to protect your body and your heart—and believe me, they are tied together!

When you decide to share your body is up to you, your heart, and your value system. But before you do share that, please talk to someone responsible you trust, and ask for ways to protect your body from an unwanted pregnancy or a sexually transmitted disease. No matter how embarrassing you may think it is, your parents are usually the best people to talk to about how to protect yourself. Having self-love makes you want to protect yourself. Self-love will help you be brave to ask someone to help you protect yourself. Protecting yourself is one of those loving choices of self-love.

Don't think getting pregnant or getting an STD can't happen to you, because it easily can. Both of those have serious consequences that will stay with you for a lifetime! More than ever judge you, your family wants to protect you and know you will always be safe and okay. You are worth the courage to ask for guidance in order to protect your body, your health, and your life! We don't want anything to happen to you that can't be undone.

If you don't feel involving your parents in this important discussion of protection is an option for you, at the very least, seek an older sibling or trusted friend who loves you and wants to protect you. Taking care of and protecting yourself is more important than your fear of asking for help. Fear is temporary, but the consequences of sex last a lifetime. If you feel you are mature enough for sex, then you must make mature decisions to protect yourself from diseases or unwanted pregnancies.

It's also your job to protect your heart, so keep developing your self-love so that you really feel and know your value. I want you to feel the value of your body and heart so you won't be quick to share them with someone who doesn't love, respect, and treasure you. You are a beautiful gift. You deserve to be treasured. You can't undo certain things in life; please let that sink in. Grow your self-love so you can become your fiercest protector. Make loving choices for yourself about who deserves your sharing your body with them. Make loving choices for yourself that will protect you from all the ways that sex can hurt you.

BRING YOUR LOVE TO THE BIG WORLD

In this world, there are lovers, selfish people, and haters. It's been my observation and experience that the "lovers" of the world are always the happiest and lead the most fulfilling lives. I hope you'll empower yourself to be one of those world lovers. Lovers are beautiful, and it's the lovers who make our world a more beautiful place for all of us to live in! They are the ones lifting up others and supporting them in loving ways. They are the people who can rise above and bring light to even dark and difficult situations. The way they love and share love almost seems to help protect them against the wrongs in the world. It's like they make love their favorite shield and weapon, and it works beautifully.

When darkness, selfishness, conflict, and hate are very present in our world, it can seem pretty overwhelming and draining. In fact, the state of our world at this moment probably has you feeling pretty overwhelmed. It's filled with people throwing stones at each other and not respecting differences of opinions, human rights, and political and religious beliefs. Those dark voices seem very loud in our world right now. This lack of understanding, love, and respect for others makes for a dark and overwhelming world around us. I know this causes you stress.

I doubt it makes you feel any better, but know that all generations in history have had to deal with dark times as part of their world. The tone of this last presidential election and the current state of our government seem like perfect examples where love of others could really make a difference. The political climate has brought out the worst in many people. Our government and politicians constantly blame one another for the state of our country. We have both the Democratic and the Republican party calling each other names and unwilling to work together to find the common good for our country as a whole. It seems there is a great lack of love and understanding for each other, but that's really what everyone wants and needs.

I know you've had to witness that darkness spread to many supporters of each of these parties too. They've been making a bad situation worse with their public feuds in the newspaper, on TV, on Twitter, on Facebook, on Instagram, in schools, in the community, at dinner tables, and so on. It seems everywhere we turn and everywhere we look, we see strong, hateful opinions and darkness in our country and big world. For those of us who value love and peace in the world, it's been stressful living in this environment and watching people bully and blame each other.

In crazy times like this, I understand the world can make you feel hopeless and helpless. It can make you feel like things will never change. I think many people feel stressed because they feel like there isn't anything they can personally do to make it better. I hope you're not one of those people. I hope you believe you can make a difference. I know you can make a difference and make it better. It requires love.

This is where bringing love to your small world can first cause a ripple effect into the big world. You can cause that and make it really matter. In times like this, we may not be able to quiet hate in our country or the world overnight, but we can begin to outnumber it and influence it with love. By doing so, you will empower others too. You can feel more in control of these hard situations by starting to improve the smaller world directly around you. If we as individuals start to bring love to where we travel each day, beginning in the kitchen each morning with our family, we will see it take root and multiply with a ripple effect. We can personally add light to many situations through love. You have to understand the power of your love really can make a difference in the world.

It will help you feel better and more empowered when you look at the smaller world around you and start your love there! If your parents are always working hard and trying their best for you, tell them thank you, and let them know you love them. If you have siblings, love them, help them, and build them up; they are your forever friends! Start with love and peace between the walls of your home. You can affect the love that happens in your home. The love that happens in your home can truly affect the world. The love that happens in your home can make you very resilient to everything else that happens to you in the world!

In your community, many people need your help and love. Some people are down on their luck or have made mistakes and find themselves hungry, homeless, or lonely and in need of a friend.

They may need love just as much as food and warm clothes if not more. Look for the people you can love in your community. Love them before they are desperate and hopeless.

It's a beautiful, powerful, and peaceful feeling to bring love to your family, friends, and neighbors. Be the kind of loving friend and loving person you need! This helps develop self-love and gives your life meaning. Take time to smile at people. Smile at the older lady who lives on your street; maybe her family has been busy and she's lonely since her husband died. Be kind, and thank the grocery store clerk because maybe people have been rude to her all day and she still has another job to go. If you can afford it, tip your waiter or waitress well, and if you can't, treat him or her with the utmost respect and friendliness. Clean out your closet, and donate clothes that can make someone's world.

If you can spare it, take some food to a shelter. Create something for a friend who has been there for you. Give someone your undivided attention. Be kind and participate positively on social media—engage and lift people up. Clean up your messes, and clean some you didn't make.

Look at people on your campus like you've never looked at them before. If you know someone with special needs, try to see his or her world and struggles, and try to help him or her feel understood and valued. Look at people who are different from you, and show them you value who they are. Look for kids who feel lonely, and help them feel seen and feel loved.

Give sincere compliments to people to build them up. Forgiveness shows love. Forgive people. Forgive yourself! Encouraging people is love. Encourage people. Encourage yourself! Be a really loving person, and look for where people need one. Don't spread gossip. Thank a police officer or military service member for his or her sacrifices and all he or she does to keep you safe. They need to feel your love.

Love your earth. Love animals. Use your time, hands, and heart to volunteer in your community. Show love to your community.

Say, "I love you," more than you ever have.

Don't just spread love in dark places. If you see light, give that love too because that light is needed more than ever! If you see someone happy, send extra love and extra smiles to him or her, because happiness takes work. It takes work to get through some of our yuck so our life thrives on all cylinders. If someone is happy, don't think it's because no one or nothing has challenged his or her happiness; everyone has struggles and obstacles. Happiness means he or she has been busy working hard and loving to get there, so love that person too!

Spread love everywhere!

Really look around at your small world because this is truly where you can make the biggest difference with your love. By empowering yourself to bring more love into your life and everyday world, you will start that powerful ripple effect into the big world. Bringing more of your love to your immediate world will bring more light to drive out darkness. Love really makes you feel you have more control in the world. Being loving will help you feel great love all around you too. The more you share love with others, the more you cultivate your self-love.

While we should give love without expecting it in return, it has been my experience that when you develop yourself in love, you will feel so much happier just from spreading love. It will come back to you in many ways. It will allow you to live more lightly and with less stress and conflict.

When you grow yourself and life with love, you drive out insecurities, hate, darkness, petty competition, comparisons, jealousy, misunderstandings, meanness, selfishness—and the list goes on. Love always brings light, beauty, strength, and hope to you, to your life, and to other people.

If every person became more aware and wanted to grow him- or herself in love and openly shared that with the people in his or her circle, the world really could be changed one person at a time. Be that person. You can grow it within yourself and then share it and watch it grow all around you with every person you touch in your life and in your travels. Your love ripples can go very far and very wide out from yourself to the rest of the world!

Love calms. Love comforts. Love excites. Love heals. Love is powerful. Love is beautiful.

Grow yourself beautiful.

GROW YOURSELF BEAUTIFUL

I have absolutely loved writing this book for you. It has truly been a labor of love. It's important to me that you know I didn't write this book because I think you're weak and can't handle life's pressures. On the contrary. I believe in your inner strength because I have seen it in my daughters and the many young women I've had experience with over the past twenty-five years. I'm continuously amazed at the strength and capabilities created within women. However, it has pained and concerned me greatly to see the harmful superficial messages coming at you from our world today, and I wanted to counteract them with truth and substance for you.

You can get manuals on how to use appliances and cars and instructional books on how to build gingerbread houses and bikes, but not on how to build the most important thing, and that's you!

In writing this book, I thought you deserved a guide with some practical advice to help you build yourself in ways I know will leave you feeling warm, strong, in charge, and beautiful.

I think girls are so precious and you will make incredibly powerful and needed contributions to our world—but all in due time. I thought you deserved to hear it's okay to slow down and take time to build your core and strong foundation. I wanted you to know how important building your foundation is so you gain the ability to succeed and handle life's twists, turns, curveballs, and crazy messages.

Anytime you feel you're headed in a stressful direction that makes you feel inadequate and not as strong and beautiful as you wish, I hope you'll pick up this book again. Every year you're older, I think you'll receive the messages a little deeper. Let it remind you that everything you need to be is already inside you—you just have to empower yourself to bring it out and put it into the sunshine so you can grow stronger and even more beautiful!

I hope this book reminds you how important it is to have loving conversations with yourself. I hope it inspires you to empower yourself to keep making loving choices for yourself so that the superficial and harmful messages become less important to you.

I've included journaling pages at the end of this book with thought starters. Journaling can have many calming, positive benefits. It's a fun way to help you sort through your feelings, understand yourself better, capture your value system, and create your dreams. Journaling can provide comfort and direction for you.

I hope every time you see a little girl in a princess dress, it'll remind you of twirling in yours. I hope it reminds you of the truth you knew way back before the world confused you—that you are the most beautiful girl in the world! I hope anytime you see a superhero, it reminds you of yourself, your incredible bravery and strength, and how much you've overcome. With each hour, day, week, month, and year, if you concentrate on what B-E-A-U-T-I-F-U-L really is and means, you will grow yourself in strength and beauty, which can never be denied by anyone ... but most importantly yourself!

Grow yourself strong. Grow yourself beautiful.

Love,

Sharon

Let's stay in touch. ♥

- **Hashtag:** #growyourselfbeautiful
- **Website:** www.sharoncaldwellpeddie.com
- **Twitter:** @SCPeddie
- **Instagram:** author_sharoncaldwellpeddie
- **Facebook page:** Author Sharon Caldwell Peddie

10
B-E-A-U-T-I-F-U-L
Journaling Pages

GROWING MYSELF BEAUTIFUL IN KINDNESS JOURNALING THOUGHT STARTERS:

- Am I kind? Do I value kindness?
- When has someone's kindness helped me through a hard time?
- How do I feel about unkind people?
- Where can I bring more kindness?

_____

_____

_____

_____

_____

_____

_____

_____

_____

_____

_____

_____

_____

_____

_____

_____

_____

GROWING MYSELF BEAUTIFUL IN EDUCATION
JOURNALING THOUGHT STARTERS:

- What areas of academics am I good at?
- What do I enjoy learning about in school? In life?
- Do I value hard work?
- Who do I admire who works hard?
- If I could be anything (even if I think I can't), what would it be?

_____

_____

_____

_____

_____

_____

_____

_____

_____

_____

_____

_____

_____

_____

_____

_____

GROWING MYSELF BEAUTIFUL IN AUTHENTICITY JOURNALING THOUGHT STARTERS:

- What causes me anxiety, sadness, and disappointment?
- What are my values, and what's important to me?
- How would someone who really knows me well describe me?
- Who are the most authentic people I know?
- What characteristics make the best kind of person and friend?
- What do I like most about myself?
- Do I spend time with people who match what I like in people?

_____

_____

_____

_____

_____

_____

_____

_____

_____

_____

_____

_____

_____

_____

_____

_____

GROWING MYSELF BEAUTIFUL BY UNPLUGGING
JOURNALING THOUGHT STARTERS:

- If I had twenty-four hours to do whatever I wanted with my time, what would I do?
- When I feel the most stressed, what are ten things I do to bring me peace?
- Where is my favorite place to get centered?
- What kind of music makes me relaxed or energized?
- Who are the people who make me feel good?
- What are at least three things each I love to see, love to smell, love to taste, and love to touch?
- If I could magically be better at ten things overnight, what would I choose?

_____

_____

_____

_____

_____

_____

_____

_____

_____

_____

_____

_____

_____

_____

_____

GROWING MYSELF BEAUTIFUL IN THANKFULNESS AND GRATITUDE JOURNALING THOUGHT STARTERS:

- What do I love about me?
- What makes me laugh?
- What are the simple, everyday things I'm grateful I'm able to do?
- What do I get to do that makes me feel free?
- Who are the people in my life I'm most grateful for?
- What are ten things in my life I wouldn't want to have to live without?
- What is going right for me?
- What do I love about my family?
- What dark time taught me the most about myself?
- What do I like about where I live?
- What are my most beautiful qualities inside and out?

GROWING MYSELF BEAUTIFUL IN RESILIENCE JOURNALING THOUGHT STARTERS:

- Do I value being tough when times are rough?
- Am I dramatic about things that end up not really mattering in the grand scheme of things?
- Am I flexible when things don't go as planned?
- Is there anything I feel stuck on that I need to move past?
- What are some of the toughest times I've made it through?
- What ten things do I do to "bounce back" when I don't want to feel knocked down?
- Do I believe in silver linings within dark life clouds?
- What are three words to describe me in the face of trouble?
- What are five things I'm most excited about right now?
- Do I accept that life will not always be easy?

_____

_____

_____

_____

_____

_____

_____

_____

_____

_____

_____

_____

_____

GROWING MYSELF BEAUTIFUL IN FAITH AND HOPE JOURNALING THOUGHT STARTERS:

- When was the last time I felt alone with a struggle?
- In what areas of my life do I have growing pains?
- What do I worry about the most?
- When times are tough, what do I do to ease my mind and heart?
- Do I believe in a higher power than myself?
- Does that higher power give me strength?
- In what area of my life do I wish I had more hope?
- Is there anything I need to tell someone but I'm scared to because I don't want to share my feelings?

_____

_____

_____

_____

_____

_____

_____

_____

_____

_____

_____

_____

_____

_____

GROWING MYSELF BEAUTIFUL IN SELF-CARE JOURNALING THOUGHT STARTERS:

- What are my ten best self-care habits?
- What areas am I most proud of in how I care for myself?
- What are my five worst self-care habits?
- Do I care for the health of my body?
- What causes me stress?
- Would I say I have good emotional health?
- Is my inner voice kind and loving to me, or does it beat me up?
- What are ten loving things I say to me and ten hurtful things I say to me?
- If I were a loving friend giving me advice, what would I say to me?
- What are five negative lies I tell myself about me that I should throw away?
- What are five to ten self-care rituals I want to add to my life?

_____

_____

_____

_____

_____

_____

_____

_____

_____

_____

_____

_____

GROWING MYSELF BEAUTIFUL IN LOVE
JOURNALING THOUGHT STARTERS:

- What do I love most about myself?
- What is most lovable about me that I wish others knew more about?
- What do I do every day that shows I have a loving, positive relationship with me?
- What do I do every day that brings love to other people even if they don't know it?
- How do I want to share more love with me? With other people?
- What situation in my life needs more love thrown at it to make it more positive?
- What people in my world deserve more of my love?

_____

_____

_____

_____

_____

_____

_____

_____

_____

_____

_____

_____

_____

_____

_____

Resources

You are never alone with your pressures, struggles, or growth process. Should you be in need, there are many great resources out there to help you, support you, and assist you in growing yourself beautiful.

- https://www.cdc.gov/family/kidsites/index.htm
- https://www.cdc.gov/HealthyYouth/sexualbehaviors
- https://www.cdc.gov/reproductivehealth/contraception/index.htm
- https://www.girlshealth.gov
- https://www.womenshealth.gov/body-image
- https://www.nimh.nih.gov/health/topics/eating-disorders/index.shtml
- https://www.nationaleatingdisorders.org/help-support/contact-helpline
- https://www.eatright.org
- https://www.nutrition.gov/subject/life-stages/teens/tweens-and-teens
- https://www.drugabuse.gov
- https://www.nimh.nih.gov/health/topics/child-and-adolescent-mental-health/index.shtml
- https://www.nimh.nih.gov/health/publications/depression-and-college-students/index.shtml
- https://suicidepreventionlifeline.org (1-800-273-8255)
- https://www.nimh.nih.gov/health/topics/suicide-prevention/index.shtml
- https://www.childmind.org/myyoungerself
- https://www.nytimes.com/guides/well/how-to-meditate

- https://health.clevelandclinic.org/how-to-use-meditation -for-teen-stress-and-anxiety
- http://www.dartmouth.edu/~healthed/relax/downloads. html#music
- https://mindfulnessforteens.com

For more information on dealing with nutrition, teen health, pregnancy prevention, STD prevention, anxiety, depression, eating disorders, OCD, and panic disorder, visit https://medlineplus.gov.

To read an article on meditation apps of 2018, visit https://www. healthline.com/health/mental-health/top-meditation-iphone-android-apps.

For more information on positive effects of Kindness:

https://www.psychologytoday.com/us/blog/emotional-nourishment /201711/why-random-acts-kindness-matter-your-wellbeing
https://www.randomactsofkindness.org/the-science-of-kindness
https://drdavidhamilton.com/the-5-side-effects-of-kindness/
https://www.youtube.com/watch?v=uhDO-JMDNJY
https://www.dartmouth.edu/wellness/emotional/rakhealthfacts.pdf

To read an article of fifteen apps to grow and inspire faith with descriptions, visit
http://www.recklesslyalive.com/15-must-have-christian-apps.

For faith-based apps for iPhone, iPad, iPod, Mac, and Android, as well as religion education, Bible, Buddhism, Hindu, LDS, Muslim, and Torah apps, and many other different kinds of religious education and prayer apps, visit these websites.

- https://support.apple.com/en-us/HT202794
- https://play.google.com

For camps and programs for teens who want to learn about God's love, visit https://www.younglife.org/Pages/default.aspx.

For more information on community service, cultural, and leadership development for girls and moms, visit https://www.nationalcharityleague.org.

Acknowledgments

First and foremost, thank you to Tom, Kelsey, Kendall, and Cami for your love and the inspiration you bring to my life. I love our close family unit so much! Thank you for believing in me and supporting me through this book journey even though I know it didn't seem like a real thing to you at first. Kelsey, Kendall, and Cami, thank you for reading the book draft and giving me your honest perspective regarding the material and its presentation. Thank you to my mom, who has always been my biggest cheerleader. You make me feel so loved, supported and capable of accomplishing anything. If heaven can hear, thank you to my dad for instilling in me the importance and satisfaction of being able to "pull myself up by the bootstraps". Thank you for taking me fishing and teaching me how to love the outdoors. I'm grateful for their healing powers.

Thank you to the young girls and young women I have had on my path. You are the motivation and inspiration for my book and a giant piece of my heart. Wisdom and advice from our older and younger generations always help light our path. Let's stick close together on our journey!

Thank you to my sister Sandy Mather and my dear friends, Tammy Austin, and Ronni Heyman for being three such intelligent, loving women in my life who I could trust to read the book and give me both honest feedback and encouragement. I treasure your genuine support in life. Thank you to my dog Maggie who literally lay at my feet for just about every hour of my writing. Writing can be an isolating experience, and your quiet companionship was just what I needed. Also, the way you looked up at me like I was writing something brilliant was especially helpful.

Thank you to my soul sisters; you know just who you are, and you get me through life. Thank you to the friends who showed great interest, asked about my book-writing process, and gave me loving encouragement. Thank you to the friends who never asked about it—it made me more determined.

Thank you to my friends near and far on Facebook who took time to encourage me anytime I gave a journey update on the book. You have no idea how comforting it felt to have people rooting for me. You also made me feel like people would care about something I had to say.

Thank you to the University of Florida and the College of Journalism for my education and for being a place of excellence and fun to belong to—I'm proud to say Go Gators! Thank you to the librarians at the University of Florida, Maggie Ansell and Colleen Seale, for allowing me to come back to my alma mater and for your help gathering valuable resources for young women who may need them on their journey.

Thank you to all of the valuable resources I was able to list at the back of my book. There are so many medical professionals and spiritual leaders doing hard, loving and important work to help others.

Thank you to the endorsers of my book who I admire for their work, compassion and strong desire to help young women grow strong and meaningfully beautiful.

Thank you to David Cole at iUniverse, who genuinely made me feel I had a great idea and a useful book in me. Thank you to iUniverse for such a professional and supportive publishing experience.

Thank you to God for all the above and the ability to write and share this book.

#growyourselfbeautiful

There is only one beautiful you.

CPSIA information can be obtained
at www.ICGtesting.com
Printed in the USA
BVHW07s1102231018
530994BV00001B/230/P